JULIUS CAESAR

Casemate Short History

JULIUS CAESAR

ROME'S GREATEST WARLORD

Simon Elliott

CASEMATE

Oxford & Philadelphia

Published in Great Britain and
the United States of America in 2019 by
CASEMATE PUBLISHERS
The Old Music Hall, 106–108 Cowley Road, Oxford OX4 1JE, UK
1950 Lawrence Road, Havertown, PA 19083, USA

Hardback Edition: ISBN 978-1-61200-709-0
Digital Edition: ISBN 978-1-61200-710-6

A CIP record for this book is available from the British Library

Printed in the Czech Republic by FINIDR, s.r.o.

Typeset in India by Versatile PreMedia Services. www.versatilepremedia.com

For a complete list of Casemate titles, please contact:

CASEMATE PUBLISHERS (UK)
Telephone (01865) 241249
Email: casemate-uk@casematepublishers.co.uk
www.casematepublishers.co.uk

CASEMATE PUBLISHERS (US)
Telephone (610) 853-9131
Fax (610) 853-9146
Email: casemate@casematepublishers.com
www.casematepublishers.com

CONTENTS

INTRODUCTION

Gaius Julius Caesar is one of the greatest figures of world history. He was both the leading politician of his day and a supreme military leader. Caesar played a crucial role in expanding Roman territory to the size that would later emerge as the Empire under his great nephew, adopted son and heir, Augustus. Later, his dramatic assassination began the terminal spiral of events that brought the Roman Republic to an end and the Empire into being.

He is known to us today by a *cognomen* that has become synonymous with power and ambition ever since. Such is the resonance of the name Caesar with political and military virility that actual titles of monarchs are derived from it. Think of the Russian and Slavic Tsar, or German Kaiser. Of course his legacy spreads far wider than simple kingship nomenclature. Think of the global spread of Latin languages and the Catholic Church, or the impact of Roman law on modern legal systems. Caesar also reformed the calendar with his Julian system, the first in Roman history to comprise 365 days. For his efforts, the Senate then named the month of July after him after his death. Few mortals can claim such an honour.

A **Roman *gens***, or clan, was an extended group of related families who shared the same *nomen* (the second personal name of a Roman citizen), could claim descent from a common ancestor, and often found common cause on the great issues of their time. In wider Roman aristocratic society one's *gens* was particularly important, especially in times of strife when members of a clan looked to each other for support.

⋙⋙⋙⋙——⋘⋘⋘⋘

Caesar was born on the 13th of July, 100 BC into the Julii clan. His family were senatorial level patricians, though they were of little renown. As a young man he owed his rapid rise along the *cursus honorum* aristocratic career path to the early death of his father when he was 16, and the conflict between the conservative pro-Senate *optimates* and reforming *populares* political factions in Rome. The former were championed by the strongman Lucius Cornelius Sulla, the latter by Caesar's uncle-in-law Gaius Marius before his death in 86 BC. When Sulla was ascendant from the late 80s BC, Caesar was frowned upon and forced to serve abroad in the military to avoid his ire. He later negotiated a return to Rome with Sulla where he then began a legal career. Caesar next travelled to Rhodes to study philosophy, and it was on this trip where he was famously captured by Cilician pirates. Once freed through the payment of a ransom, he had his captors crucified. This was not a man to be messed with. He next fought troops of the last of the Hellenistic monarchs who had the audacity to stand up to the power of Rome in the east, Mithridates VI Eupator, the king of Pontus.

Caesar later aligned himself with the next great Roman warlord, Gnaeus Pompey. This aided his progression along the *cursus honorum* and by 61 BC he was the governor of the key province of Hispania Ulterior (Further Spain). In 59 BC he became consul for the first time, later facilitating the formation of the Triumvirate alliance to control power in Rome alongside Pompey and his fabulously wealthy rival Marcus Licinius Crassus. This lifted Caesar to the top tier of Roman politics. He was then awarded the governorship of Gaul, conquering any lands initially out of Roman control between 58 and

50 BC. This included two incursions to Britain in 55 and 54 BC, the first time these islands enter the historical record.

Caesar's military success in Gaul, while popular among the military and lower classes in Rome, caused friction with his two fellow triumvirs. The upstart from the Julii was beginning to steal their thunder. Things were patched up at the conference at Luca in 56 BC, but Crassus's untimely death in 53 BC while campaigning against the Parthians started a sequence of events that saw Caesar and Pompey eventually locked into a life or death struggle. The Roman aristocracy, despite Caesar's successes abroad, increasingly saw him as an interloper threatening their traditional power. They elevated Pompey to be their champion. Caesar famously led his troops across the Rubicon river in 49 BC on his way to challenge Pompey in Rome. The latter then fled to Greece where Caesar finally defeated him at the crucial battle of Pharsalus in 48 BC. Pompey was beheaded in Egypt soon afterwards, and within two years Caesar was the sole master of the Roman world. In this period he became entangled in the politics of the Ptolemaic court in Egypt. This included his infamous affair with the queen there, Cleopatra. Now dictator for life, such events set him aloof from his noble peers in Rome with whom friction continued to grow, despite Caesar filling the Senate with allies and courting the adulation of the masses. Matters finally came to a head with his assassination in the Senate House aged 55 on the Ides of March in 44 BC at the hands of his political opponents. This event martyred him in the eyes of contemporaries, starting a final vicious round of civil wars that destroyed the Republic and created the Empire.

Given Caesar's prominence as one of the most influential figures in world history, we are fortunate that sources proliferate about his adult life. Modern ones are too numerous to mention, but in terms of primary sources the key ones include Caesar himself in his own *The Conquest of Gaul* and *Civil War*, his contemporaries Cicero in his letters and various works, Sallust in his *Catiline's Conspiracy*, Caesar's legate Aulus Hirtius who added a chapter to the *Gallic Wars* and may have edited *On the African War* and *On the Spanish War* (both narrating Caesar's activities there), Velleius and his late 1st century BC/ early 1st century AD *Roman History*, Plutarch with his early

2nd century AD *Lives*, Suetonius with his *Twelve Caesars* written in the same period, Appian with his *Roman History* in the mid-2nd century AD, Cassius Dio with his early 3rd century AD *Roman History*, and Jordanes in the 6th century AD with his *Romana.* The later 1st century BC/early 1st century AD historian Livy also wrote about Caesar, but his works do not survive other than as excerpts. It should be noted here the paucity of primary sources regarding Caesar's early family history and childhood.

A few housekeeping notes regarding this book. First, it concentrates on Caesar as a political leader and a soldier. To be a leading aristocrat in Rome was to play a never-ending series of zero-sum games where losing, either in law or war, was to risk everything. The two keys to success were rhetorical excellence and military skill. Caesar was supremely gifted at both. In the first instance, that Caesar himself recorded his own exploits illustrates a particular skill he employed, akin to that used by any leading modern politician. This was as a first-class strategic communicator. From a young age he realised that communicating his successes on his own terms, and similarly downplaying his failures, was vital to maintaining the momentum of his political and military career. In particular he excelled at identifying what today would be called the stakeholder audiences important to him at that stage in his life, and then engaging with them with the most appropriate messages. Think the political classes, lower classes, military or his military opponents. All were engaged at the time of his choosing, and with the information he wanted them to hear. That he was personally engaging and charismatic helped, as did his highly developed skills as a public speaker. Suetonius said of him, 'Caesar equalled, if not surpassed, the greatest orators and generals the world had ever known' (*The Twelve Caesars*, Julius Caesar, 55). In the same section he then goes on to quote Cicero, often critical of Caesar, in a letter to Cornelius Nepos as saying, 'Do you know any man who, even if he has concentrated on the art of oratory to the exclusion of everything else, can speak better than Caesar?'

Caesar also excelled with his military skills, both as a leader and warrior. In terms of the former he was most often victorious, but even in defeat he learnt from the experience and returned even stronger. In this regard, he presents a supreme example of that most Roman of virtues, grit. For his individual martial skill we can again turn to Suetonius (*The Twelve Caesars*, Julius Caesar, 57) who says he was a gifted swordsman and horseman, with surprising powers of endurance and who always chose to lead his armies personally, often marching on foot with his legionaries.

The chapter flow of this book is as follows. Chapter 1 addresses the Roman military machine of the late Republic, given this was so vital to Caesar's success, not only on the battlefield but also politically. Chapter 2 moves on to a short history of the Republic to the time of Sulla's First Civil War in the early 1st century BC as Caesar came of age. This will provide context for what follows. Chapter 3 then features a consideration of the Julii family and Caesar's childhood, before picking up the story of Caesar's early political and military career. Chapter 4 next looks in detail at his dramatic, eight-year conquest of Gaul including his two incursions to Britain in 55 and 54 BC. Chapter 5 then covers the subsequent civil wars that saw him campaign in Macedonia, Greece, Egypt (and there his liaison with Cleopatra), Anatolia, North Africa and Spain, through to his assassination 54 BC. The book finishes with a short conclusion that considers his legacy, both in the ancient world and subsequently.

The reader will note the use in the title, and throughout the book, of the term warlord. This might seem anachronistic given the structured nature of Roman society, but the term is very appropriate for the likes of Marius, Sulla, Pompey, Crassus and Caesar. This phenomenon at the top of Roman society was facilitated by the military reforms of Marius himself in 107 BC.

These warlords created a new kind of legion that included all of the specialists among its ranks needed to enable operations independent of long lines of supply. Such formations were therefore very mobile, allowing the new Roman warlords of the late Republic (often proconsuls governing new frontier provinces) to build private armies of multiple legions to conquer enemy territory and to fight each other. As part of his military reforms Marius also removed the property requirement to serve in the legions, opening their ranks to the lower end of Roman society. With little money of their own, such troops proved very loyal to their leaders. A particular driver here was the vast wealth of the former Hellenistic kingdoms in the eastern Mediterranean, forever drawing these warlords there in their desire to enrich themselves, their soldiers and their supporters back in Rome. The situation reached epidemic proportions by the time of the last round of civil wars, when Octavian emerged the victor, inheriting a grand total of 60 legions.

A final point here is with regard to the use of classical and modern names. The current name is used when a place or city is mentioned, and the Roman name is referenced at the first point of use. Meanwhile, where a classical name for a given post or role is well-understood, such as *legate* for general, in most instances that is used, again with the modern name in brackets at the point of first use. It is also useful here to set out the meaning of the terms consul and tribune given they play a prominent role in the narrative. A consul was highest level of magistrate in the Roman Republic, with two elected annually. They set the political policy to be followed by the Senate during their year of tenure, though given they were nominated by senators before a popular election by those entitled to vote, such policies were often aligned with those preferred by the senatorial classes. Even after the creation of other magistracies as the Republic progressed, for example tribunes, consuls still had the power of a head of state. They convened and then presided over the Senate, commanded the armies of Rome on campaign and in battle, and were the representatives of the Roman state in all foreign policy matters. Each consul had the power of veto over the other to provide some degree of political check and balance. Meanwhile, a tribune was the name of the various elected officials of Rome, with the two most important being the military tribunes and the tribunes of the plebs. A number of the former were elected each year and commanded a part of the army, serving under the consul when he commanded a larger force. The latter were introduced after the First Secession of the Plebs in 494 BC (see Chapter 2) and represented the non-patrician classes in Roman society. They were elected by plebeians only.

100 BC	Gaius Julius Caesar born
88 BC	Sulla's First Civil War
86 BC	Marius dies
85 BC	Caesar's father dies
84 BC	Caesar nominated to be the *Flamen Dialis*, marries Cornelia
83 BC	Sulla's Second Civil War
82 BC	Sulla becomes dictator, Caesar flees to Asia to join the military
78 BC	Sulla dies, Caesar returns to Rome
76 BC	Daughter Julia born
75 BC	Caesar captured by Cilician pirates while travelling to Rhodes
73 BC	Caesar appointed as one of the 15 pontiffs serving the *Pontifex Maximus*, returns to Rome
69 BC	Cornelia dies
67 BC	Marries Pompeia
65 BC	Caesar is an aedile
63 BC	Caesar elected *Pontifex Maximus*
62 BC	Caesar is a praetor, then proconsul in Hispania Ulterio
61 BC	Divorces Pompeia
60 BC	First Triumvirate.
59 BC	Caesar is consul, marries Calpurnia. His daughter marries Pompey
58 BC	Caesar campaigns against the Helvetii and Suebi
57 BC	Caesar campaigns against the Belgae
56 BC	Conference of Lucca, campaign against the Veneti, battle of Morbihan
55 BC	Massacre of the Usipetes and Tencteri, Caesar's first incursion to Britain

54 BC	Caesar's second incursion to Britain, death of his daughter Julia and mother Aurelia
53 BC	Rebellion of the Eburones and Nervii tribes in Gaul, death of Crassus
52 BC	Gallic revolt under Vercingetorix, siege of Alesia
51 BC	End of the Gallic Wars
49 BC	Caesar crosses the Rubicon river with *legio* XIII. Spanish campaign against the *optimates*
48 BC	Battle of Pharsalus, death of Pompey in Egypt
47 BC	Alexandrian War, birth of Caesarion, campaigns against Pharnaces II
46 BC	Battle of Thapsus, quadruple triumph in Rome
45 BC	Battle of Munda
44 BC	Caesar appointed dictator for life, assassinated on the Ides of March

CHAPTER 1

CAESAR'S LEGIONS

Julius Caesar was a first-class military leader who owed his success in both civilian and military life to the loyalty of the legions he led. Their actions under his command defined his career, for example, when he led the *legio* XIII *Gemina* across the Rubicon river on his way to Rome in 49 BC in defiance of the political classes of Rome. The exploits of his soldiers enthralled people across the Republic, with his *legio* X *Equestris* being the most famous military unit of his day. Whether in his campaigns of conquest or in civil wars, Caesar was never shy in raising new legions, the troops often carrying his bull symbol on their shields. In times of crisis he even raised legions from non-Romanized natives, for example *legio* V *Alaudae* in Gaul in 52 BC. Yet the story of how these warriors became the elite soldiers of the ancient world is far from straightforward. This chapter traces the development of the legionary from before the time of the Republic to Caesar's day, examining how his equipment evolved to that used by Caesar's legionaries. It then looks at Caesar's legions on campaign, before finally considering the warrior's life experiences. This will give the reader insight into how Caesar was able to attract such intense loyalty from his troops, thus enabling his success as a political and military leader.

Evolution of the Caesarian Legionary

The first insight we have into Roman military tradition comes from a time when the city was under Etruscan rule before the days of the Republic. This Etrusco-Roman army adopted the Greek-style hoplite phalanx as its main line of battle formation. This was introduced to the region when the Etruscans met the Greek colonies of southern Italy and eastern Sicily. The term phalanx references a deep formation of armoured spearmen whose front ranks fought with their long spears in an overarm thrusting position. Each front-rank warrior was protected by interlocking *aspis,* large round body shields carried by the hoplite and his neighbours. Warriors in the rear ranks added their weight to the formation and replaced those who fell in battle.

The Etrusco-Roman phalanx was supported on its flanks by Roman/ Latin troops who still fought in a loose formation as did their Villanovan ancestors. Common weapons for these troops were spears, axes and javelins. This way of fighting, with a solid phalanx of hoplites in the centre and lighter troops either side, was formalised by Servius Tullius, the first of the great reforming Roman military leaders. He instituted the Servian Constitution in the mid-6th century BC, which divided Roman society into seven different classes. Each had a different military commitment to the Roman state based on wealth. Top of the tree were the *equites*, these being the wealthiest citizens who could afford a horse and thus formed the cavalry. Next were the First Class, an Etrusco-Roman phalanx formed of 80 centuries of hoplites, followed by the Second Class of 20 centuries of spearmen with helmet, greaves and the *scutum* rectangular shield (this a generic term here rather than the later classic legionary shield). Going down the scale, next was the Third Class, comprised of 20 centuries of spearmen with helmet and *scutum*, then the Fourth Class of 20 centuries of spearmen with *scutum* only. Finally in terms of military commitment were the Fifth Class, 20 centuries of missile troops.

An equites of the Tullian legions.

This system was put to the supreme test in conflict with the Senones Gauls when, at the battle of Allia in 390 BC, it catastrophically failed. The Romans were not only defeated, but nearby Rome sacked soon after. In short order the Tullian system was dumped in favour of the much more flexible manipular system introduced by Marcus Furius Camillus. This initially featured two legions, each commanded by a consul, with six *tribuni militum* subordinates serving beneath him. These new legions numbered 3,000 men each, though this quickly increased to 6,000 over time. Within the Camillan legion there were three classes of line-of-battle troops, all called legionaries for the first time. Their classification was based on experience and age rather than wealth. The specific classes were the *triarii, principes* and *hastati*. The first were veterans wearing helmet and body armour and carrying the new *scutum* (full body shield). They were armed with the *hasta* (thrusting spear), featuring a socketed iron spearhead up to 30cm in length and a bronze butt-spike, the latter acting as a counterweight to the spearhead. Each also carried a sword. They replaced, in part, the old Tullian First Class. Meanwhile the *principes* were older warriors, also wearing helmet and body armour and carrying the *scutum*. Initially armed with the *hasta*, they replaced these with *pila* (heavy throwing javelins) of Spanish origin as the Republic progressed. These were javelins with a barbed head and a long iron shank, a lead weight sitting behind the latter in the socket where it joined the wooden shaft of the weapon. This combination gave the *pilum* tremendous penetrating power, with the shank designed to bend on impact so that even a simple hit on a shield would make the latter's use impossible. Each legionary carried two, one lighter and one heavier, the first thrown at range and the latter immediately prior to impact before swords were drawn. The *principes* also replaced, in part, the old Tullian First Class. Finally came the *hastati*, 'the flower of young men'. Again equipped with a helmet, though with less body armour, they too carried the *scutum*, initially the *hasta* and later *pila*, together with sword. They replaced the old Tullian Second class.

The Camillan legion was completed with three lesser classes of warrior. These were the *rorarii, accensi* and *leves* who replaced, sequentially, the old Tullian Third, Fourth and Fifth classes. They were support troops rather than line-of-battle troops and became less important as the Republic progressed.

The *triarii, principes* and *hastati* all formed up in a looser formation than the old Tullian phalanx. This allowed free use of the sword and *scutum*, something impossible in the dense phalanxes of old. This change was directly related to the height of the Gallic warriors faced at Allia and later by the legions of Rome, and their fighting technique. The Gauls were taller than their Roman counterparts and fought with long iron swords,

A Tullian First-Class warrior fighting an Italian hill tribesman.

utilising a downward slashing technique. This rendered the Tullian First-Class hoplite's *aspis*, designed to defend the user and his neighbours from frontal attack, less practical. The new *scutum*, thought to be of Samnite origin, was used in a much more proactive way. It could be pushed forward offensively, or raised to take the blow from an opponent's sword. The legionary would then thrust his own sword into the enemy's midriff.

The veteran *triarii* with their *hasta* did retain the ability to deploy in a dense formation if needed. They were traditionally held back in reserve (often kneeling on their right knee), and could form a hedge of spears against mounted opponents or to cover a retreat.

The original Camillan legionary *scutum* was a large curved rectangle, up to 120cm in length and 75cm in width. Made from planed wooden strips that were laminated together in three layers, the shield featured an *umbones* (iron boss) attached to the centre where the shield was slightly thicker. It was completed by fitting a calf-skin/felt facing. The legionary *scutum* was very heavy and could weigh up to 10kg, being held by a horizontal grip using a straightened arm.

For body armour Camillan legionaries of all three classes wore a square bronze pectoral covering their heart and upper chest. This was held in place with leather straps. As the Republic progressed, those who could afford it (usually *triarii* and *principes*) increasingly replaced these primitive pectorals with *lorica hamata* (chainmail shirts). Of Gallic origin and weighing up to 15kg, these offered greatly improved protection, covering the torso from shoulder to hip. They were made from interlinked

A Caesarian legionary in lorica hamata *(chainmail). (Paul Cummins)*

iron rings 1mm thick and up to 9mm in external diameter, with up to 20,000 being needed for each shirt.

This Camillan legionary defensive panoply was completed with a helmet. These were made from bronze, fitting the cranium and providing good overall protection. Popular designs included those called Etrusco-Corinthian, Attic and Montefortino.

The Camillan manipular legion deployed in three lines, the first having 15 maniples of *hastati* comprising 60 men and two officers. Each of these maniples had 20 *leves* attached to act as skirmishers. The second line comprised 15 maniples of *principes*, again each of 60 men and two officers. The third line was formed by 15 *ordines*, each *ordo* comprising a *vexilla* of *triarii*, a *vexilla* of *rorarii* and a *vexilla* of *accensi*. These *vexilla* numbered 60 warriors and two officers, with the *triarii* additionally having a standard bearer.

A final innovation of Camillus would have been very popular with Caesar's later legionaries. This was because it was he who for the first time paid the legionaries for their service. This was in the context of the long siege of the Etruscan city of Veii which ended in 396 BC. The siege was of such length that the troopers were kept away from their normal work for lengthy periods of time. To compensate, Camillus introduced a legionary *stipendium* cash allowance.

The manipular legion further evolved into what historians call the Polybian system after Rome's conflict with Pyrrhus of Epirus and his Hellenistic army in the early 3rd century BC. Polybius was the leading 2nd-century BC Greek historian who narrated the story of Rome's conflicts in the 3rd and 2nd centuries BC.

The Polybian legions were again deployed in three lines, this time featuring 1,200 *hastati* in 10 maniples of 120. Next came 1,200 *principes* organised in the same way, and finally 600 *triarii* in 10 maniples of 60. Each of the maniples featured two centurions, two subordinates and two standard bearers. The major change was the disappearance of the *leves*. These were replaced by 1,200 *velites*, specialist skirmishers divided among the other maniples. Meanwhile the *rorarii* and *accensi* also disappear at this time. The

Polybian legion also featured a formal cavalry component, 300 strong and divided into 10 *turmae* of 30 troopers. These legions, used to such great effect in three Punic Wars, four Macedonian Wars and the Roman–Seleucid War, were highly efficient and adaptable. For example, they learned from their three defeats in Italy in the 2nd Punic War and ultimately beat Hannibal at the battle of Zama in 202 BC and thus won the conflict.

The main weapon of the Polybian *principes* and *hastati* – and side arm of the hasta-armed *triarii* – was the *gladius Hispaniensis* sword. A new innovation in the Polybian legions, its use was ubiquitous by the mid-3rd century BC. It was to remain the standard legionary sword through to the time of Caesar and beyond. The weapon was of Spanish origin, and rather than being the short stabbing sword of popular legend, it was instead a cut and thrust design up to 69cm long and 5cm in width. The *gladius* featured a tapering sharp stabbing point and was worn on the right-hand side unless by an officer. Those legionaries who could afford it would also carry a *pugio*, a 30cm long dagger. The Polybian *principes* and *hastati* also carried two *pila* in the same manner as their Camillan forebears, one heavy and one light. Meanwhile the *triarii* continued to use the *hasta*.

For defensive equipment all three classes of Polybian legionary carried the *scutum*, helmet, armour of some kind for the upper torso and often also the lower legs. The shield was the same as the earlier Camillan design, while more and more legionaries wore the *lorica hamata*. If the legionary could afford it, he also wore an iron or bronze greave on the leading left lower leg, or both legs for the very well off. Meanwhile, a new innovation was made with regard to the helmet. As the Republic progressed and the legionaries came into continued contact with the Gauls and later Galatians, two new types appeared. These were the Coolus design with a round cap of bronze and small neck guard, and the iron Port type with a deep neck guard. The latter developed into the classic 'Imperial' Gallic helmet often associated with the Principate Roman legionary of the 1st and 2nd centuries AD. Etrusco-Corinthian, Attic and Montefortino designs continued to be used by the Polybian legionary, but most had disappeared by the beginning of the 1st century BC.

The final reforms of the legions prior to Caesar's day were those carried out by Marius, who completely reorganised the Roman military establishment in 107 BC. His aim was to turn each individual legion into a self-contained fighting force. To do this he standardised the legionary on the *gladius* and *pilum*-armed *principes* and *hastati* (these terms now being dropped), with the spear-armed *triarii* and javelin-armed *velites* disappearing entirely. From this point, all of the fighting men in the legion were simply called legionaries, numbering 4,800 out of a total 6,000 men in each legion. The remaining 1,200 troopers were support personnel who carried out a wide variety of roles which enabled the legion to function autonomously.

Marius also replaced the old Camillan and Polybian manipular system with centuries, each comprising 80 legionaries and 20 support staff, sub-divided into units of 10 (eight legionaries and two non-combatants). Each century was commanded by a centurion, who each had specific titles which reflected their seniority based on the old Camillan and Polybian manipular legions. The names, with seniority in ascending order, were:

- *hastatus posterior*
- *hastatus prior*
- *princeps posterior*
- *princeps prior*
- *pilus posterior*
- *pilus prior*

The legionaries lived, fought and ate together, with each legion developing their own identity around the new *aquila* (eagle standards) introduced by Marius. Training was also regularised, with Marius insisting on regular fitness drills to ensure the legionaries were always physically fit. This was to ensure the legionary could carry his own equipment on campaign, with the troops earning the nickname *muli mariani* (Marius' mules). One should perhaps envision the Marian legionary as having the same body shape as a 165cm tall modern Olympic weightlifter, square and all muscle. His training particularly focused on martial skills, based on the methods used to instruct gladiators. As an example, for sword drill, a large stake the size of an opponent was set up in the training ground. The trooper then practiced his *gladius* and *scutum*-based fencing technique using a wooden replica sword and wicker shield, with the stake being 'the enemy'.

The main advantage of the new Marian legions, as detailed in the Introduction, was that they didn't have to rely on long lines of supply given they were self-contained units with integral specialists. This allowed late Republican warlords like Caesar and Pompey to amalgamate a large number into huge armies owing their loyalty to a specific leader, especially when campaigning on the frontiers of the growing Republic well away from Rome. In such circumstances it became common for the various warlords to actually raise their own legions without the approval of the Senate, often using their own or supporter's money to finance them.

In terms of equipment, these Marian legionaries were all equipped in the same way, with *scutum*, *lorica hamata*, Coolus and Port type helmets, two *pila*, the *gladius* and the *pugio*. By doing away with differentially armed troop types within the legions, Marius therefore made them much easier to maintain in the field.

The standard deployment in battle for the Marian legions, including those of Caesar and Pompey, remained the three lines of the earlier manipular system. The first two were deployed to sequentially engage the enemy (second line units replacing the front-line units as the latter tired), while the third acted as a reserve, just as the *triarii* had in the manipular legions. Caesar himself provides direct insight into this tactical approach, describing how when fighting the supporters of Pompey in Spain in 49 BC he deployed four cohorts of legionaries in his front line and three in the second and third.

Caesar's Legions on Campaign

Caesar was a very shrewd political and military operator who knew that he could only achieve his personal ambitions if backed by loyal legions. His campaigns in Gaul from 58 to 50 BC, and later in the civil war against Pompey and his supporters from 49 to 45 BC, are excellent examples of this. Many of these legions were founded under his leadership, and went on to have long and successful careers well into the Principate Empire.

Caesar was particularly adept at accruing legions to ensure weight of numbers told in his favour. For example, when given the governorship in Gaul in 59 BC he inherited four legions. These were legions VII, VIII, IX and X, the latter effectively his own personal legion. This was because it was the first he had personally founded, in 61 BC when governor of Hispania Ulterior. He later named it *Equestris* (mounted) after famously mounting some of its legionaries in a bid to fool the German King Ariovistus during a parley in 58 BC (see Chapter 4).

At the time of Caesar's accession to the governorship of Gaul these four legions were deployed defensively in northern Italy, given the early province here only included Cisalpine Gaul (modern northern Italy) and a strip of territory along the coast linking it with Spain. The latter was called Provincia, the root of the modern name for the region, Provence. Also called Transalpine Gaul at the time, it later became the Imperial province of Gallia Narbonensis.

With destiny calling, Caesar immediately set his sights on conquering the remainder of Gaul in the name of Rome. He was keenly aware of the difficulty of the task and immediately began recruiting new legions before launching his first offensive north of the Alps in 58 BC. These new legionaries were most often Roman citizens recruited in Cisalpine Gaul. His first new legions here were legions XI and XII in 58 BC, then *legio* XIII *Gemina* and *legio* XIV in 57 BC, *legio* XIV again in 53/ 52 BC after it had been destroyed, *legio* XV in 53/ 52 BC and finally the native Gallic *legio* V *Alaudae* and also *legio* VI in 52 BC.

Caesar first shows an ability to concentrate his legions into a single striking force in his Gallic campaigns. For example, all eight of his then extant legions were involved when fighting the Belgic Nervii near the River Sambre in 57 BC. Caesar also made use of the tactical flexibility of the Marian legions during his Gallic campaigns. For example he only took legions VII and X to Britain during his first incursion in 55 BC, with the other six left in Gaul as a garrison. When he returned to Britain in 54 BC with a point to prove, he still only took five of his eight legions. In these Gallic campaigns the legions would have stayed in marching camps built at the end of every day's march when in enemy territory, later being dispersed among friendly (at least ostensibly) Gallic *oppida* during the winter months.

Caesar again showed his propensity for recruiting new legions, often against the wishes of the Senate, during his civil war with Pompey and his supporters. This began in 49 BC when he crossed the Rubicon river just south of Ravenna, traditionally the boundary between Cisalpine Gaul and Italy proper, with *legio* XIII *Gemina*. The bold move, fully detailed in Chapter 4, disconcerted the political classes of Rome, and their champion Pompey fled to Greece. Caesar then set about building up his power base in Italy. He was already able to field

Gallic allied cavalry as used by Caesar in his Gallic and civil war campaigns.

legions V to XV, which he used to defeat Pompey's supporters in Spain in later 49 BC. He then made full use of his unchallenged access to the recruiting grounds of Italy. As consul in 48 BC he recruited legions I, II, III and IV. He then began extending the sequence past XV, possibly up to *legio* XXX. This gave him an enormous number of troops to command. He ultimately led them to victory over Pompey in later 48 BC, and his supporters by 45 BC.

Talk of leadership brings us onto Caesar's personal relationship with his legionaries. In that regard he was a first-class leader of men, both at a strategic level when planning and effecting his campaigns, and tactically when fighting his battles. This reflected his skill as a communicator, naturally knowing how to engage subordinates of all levels to ensure victory. The most extreme form of this would be leading his men from the front at crucial times in the heat of battle, *scutum* raised and *gladius* in hand. As Suetonius explains, 'If Caesar's troops gave ground he would often rally them in person, catching individual fugitives by the throat and forcing them round to face the enemy again' (*The Twelve Caesars*, Julius Caesar, 62). He later adds, 'He always addressed his soldiers not with "My men", but with "Comrades" … which put them into a better humour' (*The Twelve Caesars*, Julius Caesar, 67).

Caesar was certainly a man of the people, at least when it came to his soldiers, and this committed engagement paid dividends throughout his many years of campaigning when he was always able to rely on their dedication and devotion. As Plutarch explains, 'He could so count on the goodwill and zeal of his soldiers, that those who in other campaigns had been in no way superior to the rest were invincible and irresistible when facing any danger on behalf of Caesar's glory' (*Lives*, Caesar, 16).

A final short consideration here are the auxiliary troops who completed the military forces deployed by Caesar in his campaigns across the Republic and beyond. Their complement would have depended on whether the theatre of engagement was in the western or eastern Mediterranean, but could have included heavy Gallic, Spanish and Macedonian cavalry, light Numidian and Syrian cavalry, Gallic and Ligurian warriors, Hellenistic thureophoroi spearmen, Spanish, Illyrian and Thracian loose order foot, and skirmishing foot from Gaul, Germany, Spain, the Balearic isles, Numidia, Macedonia, Greece and Crete.

There is some debate about whether Caesar also used war elephants. These beasts of war had first been encountered by Rome when fighting Pyrrhus in the early 3rd century BC, and later in the Punic Wars and when fighting the Hellenistic kingdoms and the Numidians. They were soon adopted by mid- and late-Republican Roman armies, and are even recorded being used in early Imperial Roman armies (see below). The 2nd century AD Macedonian author Polyaenus (*Stratagems*, 8.23.5) records that Caesar had one large elephant when campaigning in Britain, which he used to force a crossing over a large river, often identified as the River Thames. Caesar himself doesn't mention this, which, given his obsession with prestige, is telling, and most historians don't give the reference any credit. Polyaenus was most likely either confusing his source material with Claudius's successful AD 43 invasion when elephants are certainly recorded arriving with the Emperor prior to the submission of the regional British tribes engaged, or was using 'Caesar' to directly refer to Claudius.

During his Thapsus campaign in North Africa in 46 BC Caesar did actually obtain elephants from Italy, using them to train his troops in how to engage the beasts. However, these are not thought to have been trained war elephants and may have been animals originally destined for the arena. Caesar subsequently captured Pompey's elephants after defeating him at Pharsalus in 48 BC, the elephants having been supplied by the latter's Numidian ally Juba. These are last mentioned at the battle of Mutina in 43 BC after Caesar's death. It is of course possible Caesar was going to take these elephants to Parthia with him where he next intended to campaign. However, war elephants were always a double-edged sword in the ancient world, difficult to control and expensive to maintain. Often a bigger threat to their own troops than the enemy, it seems likely that the pragmatic Caesar distrusted them and preferred to rely on his legionaries and supporting auxiliaries.

The Life of Caesar's Legionaries

Until the reforms of Marius, the Camillan and Polybian manipular legions were formed by a compulsory levy of Roman citizens who met a minimum wealth/property qualification. These formations were raised whenever necessary rather than being forces in being. Recruitment into their ranks was usually authorised by the Senate, with the legion later being disbanded once the need for its existence had passed.

A key aspect of Marius's reforms in 107 BC was to realise that, given Rome's by then widespread military responsibilities, this early Republican system was no longer sustainable. He determined that standing units were required that could remain in existence for years or even decades, and thus were born the Marian legions. To man these he principally relied on volunteer recruits usually aged between 17 and 23, though some were as young as 13 and or as old as 36. Additionally, in times of crisis, the number of legionaries was bolstered by conscription under a levy called the *dilectus*.

Each legionary, whether recruit or conscript, signed up for a minimum term of six years. This length of service lasted until at least the battle of Actium in 31 BC. Land was also offered to them upon their retirement and the veterans often settled in colonies. Caesar provides a good example – his retirees after the campaign in Greece against Pompey settled at the Hellenistic city of Butrint (Roman *Buthrōtum*) in modern Albania.

Marius also abolished the wealth/property requirement, and from that point the majority of recruits came from the landless lower classes. This was a shrewd move that increased the sense of identity within each individual legion, with the legionaries now increasingly 'other' when compared to the rest of society. At

Butrint, the Hellenistic town in modern Albania where Caesar settled his veteran troops after fighting Pompey in the Pharsalus campaign of 48 BC.

a stroke the warlords of the later Empire were therefore able to wield armies that owed more loyalty to them than to the Senate and people of Rome.

Caesar was ever sensitive to the needs of his legionaries and increased their pay to 225 denarii a year, a sure means of ensuring their loyalty. It is unclear if his opponents immediately copied the move, but this amount became standard legionary pay through to the time of the Emperor Domitian in the late 1st century AD. Plutarch (*Lives*, Caesar, 17) adds that Caesar was also adept at spreading the plunder from his campaigns among his troops. He always went out of his way to ensure he didn't appear to be amassing wealth for his own ends.

Like all armies, Caesar's legions marched on their stomachs. Later the 4th century AD writer Vegetius said in his military manual that troops should never be without corn, salt, wine and vinegar and that would certainly have been the case for Caesar's legions, with beans, bread, porridge, vegetables and eggs forming the core diet. Meat would be added on feast days, with the wider diet supplemented by local produce and hunting. On campaign, as Caesar's legions so often were, the daily staples

The city walls of Butrint in modern Albania, where Caesar settled his veterans. Roman legionaries were also highly skilled engineers who built fortifications across the Roman Republic and later Empire.

were whole-wheat biscuits and hard tack, together with bread baked in the marching camp at the end of the day's march.

Religion was a key feature in the daily lives of Caesar's legionaries, playing a major role in their appreciation of belonging and belief. Roman society, within the military and without, was very conservative and in that regard each legionary was obliged to honour the gods of the Roman pantheon, in particular the Capitoline triad of Jupiter, Juno and Minerva given their association with Rome. We can add to these Mars, given he was the god of war. The worship of gods associated with a given

The Capitoline Triad of Jupiter, Juno and Minerva. Religion played a great part in Caesar's life, both professional and private.

legion's place of origin, often a local deity assimilated into the Roman pantheon in some way, was also common.

For non-military kit all of Caesar's legionaries carried their equipment on a T-shaped pole resting on their shoulders when on the march, with the shield held in place across the back. Helmets were usually strung from the neck across the chest. The marching kit also included a *paenula*, a hooded, woollen bad weather cloak made from thick wool that fastened with a button or toggles on the centre of the chest. The officers wore a shorter rectangular cloak called a *sagum* which fastened on the right shoulder with a brooch.

A very important piece of kit for the legionary, including Caesar himself when minded to march with his troops, were the hobnailed *caligae* (sandals). Typically these featured a leather upper made from a single leather piece which was sewn at the heel. This was then stitched to a multiple-layer hide sole shod with many iron studs, each sandal weighing up to 1kg. Caesar's legionaries also carried a sturdy cross-braced satchel for their personal effects, a water skin in a net bag, a *patera* (bronze mess

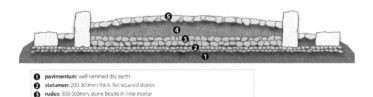

1. **pavimentum:** well rammed dry earth
2. **statumen:** 200-300mm thick, flat squared stones
3. **rudus:** 300-500mm, stone blocks in lime mortar
4. **nucleus:** 300mm, concrete with sand , crushed stones, broken tiles or other local materials
5. **summum dorsum:** 200-250mm, cobbles or slabs in mortar

Roman legionary engineering expertise. A cross-section of a Roman road built by Roman legionaries. (Paul Baker)

tin), a cooking pot, canvas bags for grain rations, spare clothing, and bespoke engineering equipment.

This brings us onto the engineering prowess of Caesar's legionaries. In the first instance every Marian legion included 1,200 specialists within the overall complement of 6,000. These included individuals with a very wide range of crafts and artisan skills, many engineering in nature. They included land surveyors, land levellers, quantity measurers, ditch diggers, master builders, glaziers, smiths, coppersmiths, wagon makers, roof-tile makers, water engineers, plumbers, masons, woodcutters, lime burners and charcoal burners. These were all called *immunes* as they were exempted from general duties. It is these specialists who were able to facilitate Caesar's great engineering feats in the field, for example the bridges over the River Rhine and siege lines at Alesia detailed in Chapter 4.

Meanwhile, Caesar's legionaries themselves were skilled engineers in their own right, able to support the specialists in the legion with any task ordered. Each of the front-line legionaries, as part of their personal engineering equipment, carried a saw, stake, chain, pickaxe, sickle, basket and leather strap. Such construction and engineering work often involved backbreaking physical hard labour, and is a further example of the fitness of the soldiers of the Marian legions.

CHAPTER 2

THE ROMAN REPUBLIC

Julius Caesar was very much a product of the Roman Republic. Its traditions and institutions shaped his life, even when he was trying to free himself of those he found most onerous to his own ambitions. A chronological knowledge of the Republic is therefore very useful in providing context for the events of his own time.

Rome Before the Republic

The origins of the Roman Republic are shrouded in myth. The most familiar founding story is that concerning the twins Romulus and Remus. In the tale they were born in the Latin town of Alba Longa to the vestal virgin Rhea Silvia. She was the daughter of a former king, Numitor, who had been usurped and imprisoned by his brother Amulius. It was the latter who forced Rhea Silvia to become a Vestal after taking the crown. She conceived the twins when visited by Mars in a sacred grove dedicated to the God of War. Amulius ordered the twins killed and so their mother abandoned them on the banks of the River Tiber. There they were saved by the river God Tiberinus. The story then says the twins were suckled by a she-wolf in a cave later called the Lupercal. They were eventually adopted by a shepherd called Faustulus, growing to manhood unaware of their aristocratic origins. However, their natural leadership qualities came to the fore and through a series of escapades they became aware of their own identities, later helping restore their grandfather to his throne. They then decided to build their own settlement on the banks of the Tiber and chose the site which later became Rome. The twins then fell out over which of the seven hills they should build the new town on, Romulus preferring the Palatine Hill and Remus the Aventine Hill. When Romulus claimed divine support for his choice, violence broke out and Remus was killed. Romulus then founded Rome on the Palatine, the date for this event set by Roman annalists as 21st April, 753 BC.

This dramatic legend had to be reconciled with another great founding myth of Rome however. This was set much earlier, in the context of the Trojan War. Here the Trojan refugee Aeneas escaped to Italy following the fall of Troy, landing near Anzio south of Rome with his followers after a series of adventures across the Mediterranean. After defeating local opposition his son Iulus, namesake of the later Julio-Claudian family, founded Alba Longa and established the line of kings which bridged the gap between the Trojan Wars and Rome's ultimate founding. The Roman poet Virgil later merged both stories in his 1st century BC epic *The Aeneid*, one of Rome's greatest literary works.

Rome's location was crucial to its subsequent rise to global dominance. The original settlement was one of a number built on the hilltops on the left bank of the Tiber at its lowest crossing point. The river is one of two major waterways rising in Apennine Mountains that bisect Italy, flowing south into the Tyrrhenian Sea. The other river is the Arno which flows west into the same sea. The region between the two was called Etruria, ranging from Pisa in the north to Ostia (the port of Rome) in the south. It was home to the Villanovan Iron Age culture from around 900 BC that, by the early 7th century BC, had evolved into the Etruscan culture. This was centred on powerful city-states, for example Veii, Caere and Tarquinii.

The influence of the Etruscans spread rapidly, mainly because of their seafaring skills. Soon a mercantile empire had been established in the western Mediterranean. Through this they came into contact with the Greek colonies in southern Italy and eastern Sicily, and also the Phoenicians of the Punic Empire in North Africa. As detailed in the previous chapter, it is from the former that they adopted the Greek hoplite phalanx as their principle line-of-battle formation. This gave the Etruscans a crucial advantage as they cast their gaze south to the settlements on the banks of the Tiber, including Rome. This was a region called Latium, which soon fell under Etruscan control.

From that point on, an Etrusco-Roman king governed Rome. It is the second of these, Servius Tullius who reigned from 575 BC to 535 BC, that instituted the Servian Constitution detailed in Chapter 1. This created Rome's first formalised military system. By the mid-6th century BC, Etruscan power had reached its height, with much of Campania below Latium, including many of the Greek settlements of Magna Graecia, conquered. Crucially though they failed to capture the Greek regional capital at Cumae with its fortified acropolis. This went on to form the centre of regional resistance to the Etruscans who were defeated in battle in 524 BC. This emboldened the other conquered settlements. Those in Latium then formed the Latin League which, fighting alongside the free Greek settlements of Magna Graecia, began to drive the Etruscans back northwards to their home territory in Etruria.

Rome's rise to prominence in Latium happened at this time. It soon became the principle town there under the command of Tarquin the Proud who was king from 534 BC to 509 BC. However, towards the end of his reign he became increasingly unpopular with the aristocracy who expelled him in 509 BC. Thus was born the Roman Republic. It is in the context of this dramatic event that we have the famous tale of Horatio and his two companions holding the last bridge over the River Tiber against Etruscans trying to fight their way back into Rome to help put Tarquin back on the throne. Their sacrifice proved worthwhile, with Tarquin the last Roman king.

The Republic is Born

The new Republic now came under the control of the great families of Rome, called patricians after the latin word *patres* (father). Only members of these great houses could hold religious or political office, particularly in the Senate where the wealthiest members of the aristocracy processed legislation under the authority of two annually elected consuls. The senatorial class made up the top tier of the three 'leisure classes' of the nobility in Rome, they being endowed with 'moral excellence', wealth and high birth. They displayed this by wearing the broad purple stripe on their togas. Next was the equestrian class, with slightly less wealth but still with a reputable lineage, these wearing the narrow purple stripe on their togas. Finally there was the curial class, again with the bar set slightly lower. The latter were largely mid-level landowners and merchants.

All Roman citizens below the senatorial class, including the equestrian and curial nobility, were called plebeians. They had no political authority, even though many were wealthy. Tensions between the two classes grew quickly, particularly as it was the poorer residents of Rome who provided the bulk of the recruits for the army. Matters came to a head in 494 BC when the plebeians went on strike, gathering outside Rome and refusing to move until granted representation. This famous event was called the First Secession of the Plebs. The risky move worked, against the odds, and the plebeians were rewarded with an assembly of their own called the *Concilium Plebis* (Council of the Plebs). This body was granted a degree of oversight of the legislation proposed by the consuls and enacted by the Senate. In this way, while the government of the Republic was certainly not democratic (for example excluding all women from any public office), it was more so than the hated monarchy that preceded

The Italian hills of the Apennines in central Italy where hill tribesmen fought warriors of the early Republic.

it. This was increasingly an important part of the Roman psyche and was certainly a card played by the opponents of Caesar when he became dictator.

The early Republic spent much of the 5th century BC battling external threats. First up was the Latin War where Rome fought its erstwhile Latin League partners from 498–493 BC. Though Rome was victorious in the main engagement at the battle of Regallus in 496 BC, it had to acknowledge its Latin neighbours as equals in the Cassian Treaty which brought the conflict to an end.

With Etruscan power waning, the Latin League then spent the next 50 years fighting off repeated raiding by a variety of hill tribes from the Apennines. These included the Aequi, Sabini, Umbri and Volsci. Increasingly squeezed out of their own lands and onto the coastal plains of Latium by the expanding Samnites of south-central Italy, in the mid-5th century BC the hill tribes burst into southern Italy and conquered Campania, Apulia and Lucania. The fight back was led by the Latin towns, with the Aequi being defeated in 431 BC and the Volsci driven back into the Apennines. Peace then descended on the region as the Latin League consolidated its control over central and western Italy.

Etruscans and Gauls

Peace was not to last. To the north the Etruscans remained a threat and another war broke out, with Rome investing the key Etruscan city of Veii in 404 BC. So began the long eight-year siege which led to Camillus paying his legionaries for the first time. Veii finally fell in 396 BC, this proving to be the high point for Roman foreign policy in the first half of the 4th century BC. That was because their next opponents were the Senones Gauls of Brennus from northern Italy. Celts from central Europe had been settling in the Po Valley there for over a century, challenging the Etruscans. The latter had established Bologne (Etruscan *Felsina*) as their principle city in the region. The riches of Etruria proved too big a draw for the Gauls and they marched south, sweeping all before them. Brennus, his warriors enriched with plunder, then targeted Latium. Rome deployed its legions, expecting a quick victory, but its army was annihilated at the battle of Allia in 390 BC. Rome was then sacked, prompting the building of the city's first defensive circuit in the form of the 11km Servian Walls after the Gauls were paid to leave.

It was in the midst of the grinding siege of Veii that the leading patrician Camillus was appointed as consular tribune to command the army in 401 BC. It was he who raised taxation to pay his troops, in so doing re-balancing the books of the Roman treasury. As seen in Chapter 1, it was also he who introduced the manipular system in response to the shock of defeat at the hands of the Gauls. This is a supreme example of the grit displayed on frequent occasions by Rome, responding to catastrophic defeat by innovating a new military system fit for purpose in the expanding world the city now found itself at the centre of.

The new Camillan military system was quickly tested against the Etruscans to the north again. Through the mid-4th century

BC Rome and her Latin League partners fought a series of increasingly brutal wars against the Etrurian city-states who were now fighting for survival. The final assault took place in 351 BC when Etruscan resistance in southern Etruria was finally broken, with Bologne in the north then falling to the Gauls in 350 BC. Its common enemy defeated, the Latin League now turned on itself and a final struggle for dominance began. Rome again emerged as the victor, now controlling all of western Italy from northern Campania to southern Etruria.

War with the Samnites

The city's next opponent were the Samnites. The Oscan-speaking people were well used to fighting in the rough terrain of their homelands and had initially been an ally of the Latin League against the hill tribes of the Apennines. However, a long series of wars broke out with Rome in 343 BC which lasted for 50 years. This included the famous Roman defeat at the Caudian Forks in 321 BC. Here, in a pass near Caudium (the capital of the Samnite Caudini tribe) both Roman consuls led their combined armies into a trap where their whole force was captured. Every man was forced to pass under a 'yoke' formed from three spears. A peace favourable to the Samnites followed.

Typically, Rome never forgave the Samnites for this humiliation. Within five years the 'Caudine Peace' had broken down and hostilities were again renewed. Once more the Samnites were for the most part victorious, but again showing grit Rome refused to accept defeat and fought back every time. The Samnites finally sued for peace in 304 BC, but again this was short lived, only lasting six years.

The Samnites then launched a full out assault on Rome in 296 BC, aiming to settle matters once and for all. They gathered a coalition of allies including Gauls, the remaining Etruscan city-states and Umbrian hill tribesmen. Once more they were initially successful, but ultimately lost the crucial Battle at

Sentinum in 295 BC. Here, only the Gauls turned up to support them and the defeat marked the end of Samnite resistance to Rome's southward expansion. It was also the death knell of the Etruscans, all their remaining city-states now falling under Roman control.

Rome's regional dominance continued to grow and the city next turned its attention to northern Italy where the Gauls were still dominant. Population pressure here was causing friction with Rome on its northern border. This was because in the early 280s BC a large-scale migration had taken place of the Gallic peoples of central Europe. Huge tribal groupings began to head eastwards, ultimately founding the Galatian kingdoms of central Anatolia after ravaging Greece, and south into Italy. The Senate decided to settle things before a full invasion of Roman territory took place and in 284 BC a 13,000 strong Roman army marched north to challenge the Gauls. Disaster again followed, and the legions were massacred at the battle of Arretium. Their commander, Lucius Caecilius Metellus Denter, was among the dead. As usual the Romans once more refused to admit defeat and launched a massive counter-strike into the heart of Gallic territory in the Po Valley. This time they were successful, evicting the whole Senones tribe out of Italy. Another Gallic tribe, the Boii, then started raiding Roman-controlled Etruria but were fought to a standstill, eventually suing for peace. This broke the last effective Gallic resistance in the north of Italy which now came under Roman control.

Pyrrhus and Hannibal

The city on the banks above the River Tiber now controlled most of the Italian peninsula, excepting the Greek cities of the south. They now became the next object of Roman attention when the Senate tried to force them into an alliance. This was quickly rebuffed, with Taranto (the leading naval power on the peninsula) appealing for help from the Hellenistic king Pyrrhus of Epirus on the western coast of the Balkans. A relation of Alexander the Great, he responded by crossing the Adriatic in 280 BC with an army 25,000 strong. These were crack troops who, as detailed in Chapter 1, fought in the Hellenistic military tradition. The force included pikemen fighting 16 deep with 6m long pikes, shock cavalry armed with *xyston* lances and, most shockingly for the Romans, war elephants.

Pyrrhus of Epirus, the Hellenistic king who was one of the greatest foes of the Roman Republic.

When word reached Rome that Pyrrhus was recruiting allies from its enemies across the Italian peninsula, the legions marched south to intercept. The first of three major battles followed at Heraclea, this proving a bruising experience for the Romans. Pyrrhus won, though at great loss, hence the phrase Pyrrhic Victory. Two further battles occurred at Asculum in 279 BC and Beneventum in 275 BC, the first another narrow Epirot victory and the second a Roman success. Pyrrhus left Italy soon after. One result of this conflict was the evolution of the Camillan manipular system into Polybian system.

Roman expansion now began to take on an international flavour. In 272 BC Taranto was captured, providing Rome with its first effective maritime capability. This led to an inevitable clash with Carthage, the regional superpower in the western Mediterranean. The First Punic War started in 264 BC, the trigger being an argument over control of the key Sicilian city of Messina. The war lasted through to 241 BC and included the battle of Agrigentum on the south coast of Sicily in 261 BC where Rome defeated the Carthaginians for the first time in battle. However, the war was largely naval in nature and here the Romans displayed their innate skill at adopting the tactics and technology of their opponents. They started the conflict as maritime underdogs but copied the Carthaginian's expertise at sea to the extent that they ultimately won the naval war and thus the whole conflict. Under the peace treaty Carthage evacuated Sicily and also paid a huge indemnity to Rome.

Peace was again short lived. The Second Punic War broke out in 218 BC and lasted 17 years, testing Rome's powers of endurance to their very limit. At the outset the Roman fleet cut off the Punic North African homeland from its key colonies in Spain. The Carthaginians were led this time by the brilliant general Hannibal. He responded with an audacious plan to invade Italy itself from Spain through southern Gaul and the Alps. The lightning campaign caught the Romans completely off guard and he defeated the legions three times at the Trebia in 218 BC, Lake Trasimene in 217 BC and Cannae in 216 BC.

The latter was a battle of titanic scale with 50,000 Carthaginians facing 86,000 Romans. Hannibal here completed his famous double envelopment of the Roman battle line, massacring 50,000 legionaries and allied troops. Many opponents would have ended the conflict after such a disaster, but not Rome. New legions were raised, two comprised of freed slaves. Crucially, Hannibal failed to capture Rome itself and was ultimately pinned down in southern Italy where attempts to re-supply him from North Africa and Spain failed, largely due to Roman naval power. Then in 204 BC Rome went on the offensive, with the consul Publius Cornelius Scipio (later Africanus) landing in the Carthaginian heartland near Tunis with a large force of 25,000. These legions and their Numidian allies decisively defeated Hannibal at the battle of Zama in 202 BC, peace soon following under the most onerous terms for the Carthaginians.

Again the peace didn't last, largely due to the Romans viewing their encounters with Carthage as unfinished business. The Senate now had grand designs on new foreign territories in Spain and Africa and the Third Punic War broke out in 146 BC with Carthage backed into a corner by the escalating demands of its conqueror. A very one-sided affair, Carthage quickly succumbed. The city itself was destroyed, with 50,000 of its citizens being sold into slavery. Rome was now master of the western Mediterranean, with Sicily, Sardinia and Corsica, the Balearic Islands, Spain and North Africa under its direct control.

Wars with the Hellenistic Kingdoms

Roman attention now turned to the eastern Mediterranean and the kingdoms created when the empire of Alexander the Great was divided after his death. First, the Macedonian King Philip V had unwisely been caught trying to make an alliance with Hannibal when the latter was still in Italy. Soon the First Macedonian War began, followed by three more that finally saw Macedonia become a Roman province in 146 BC. Rome was also victorious fighting the over-confident Seleucid monarch Antiochus III in the Seleucid-Rome War. These campaigns featured a number of enormous set piece battles between legion and phalanx. The key ones were Cynoscephalai in 197 BC where Philip V was defeated during the Second Macedonian War, Magnesia in 190 BC when Antiochus III was defeated in western Anatolia, and Pydna in 168 BC when the new Macedonian king Perseus was defeated.

The final resistance to Roman hegemony in Greece came in 146 BC when the Achaean League in the northern and central Peloponnese declared war on Rome. The ensuing Achaean War was a short-lived affair, the Achaeans being totally defeated and the leading city Corinth sacked and raised to the ground.

Rome was now the undoubted super power in the Mediterranean, its legions triumphant across the region. One result of its spectacular success against the Hellenistic kingdoms was that fabulous amounts of loot and plunder were now making their way to Rome, enriching army commanders and troops alike. It should be remembered that when Alexander the Great finally defeated the Achaemenid Persian in the later 4th century BC, the Macedonian conquerors inherited the vast wealth of this huge empire. Following the Wars of the Successors after his

Trireme war galleys such as this example played a key role in the naval campaigns fought across the Mediterranean by the Roman Republic.

death this was spread out among the various successor states, particularly the Macedonian, Seleucid and Ptolemaic kingdoms of the eastern Mediterranean. This is what fell into Rome's lap, dwarfing the riches amassed after the defeat of Carthage. The aristocracy back in Rome could now see fortunes were to be made in the east through military conquest, which from this point proved an enormous draw. This began to cause friction among the nobility as they vied for control of the campaigning forces and soon a new type of military leader emerged, the late republican warlord detailed in the introduction and Chapter 1. It was this development more than anything that set the Republic on the path to its demise a century later.

A Macedonian warrior with a pike and star-patterned shield. The legionaries of the Roman Republic made short work of Macedonian pike phalanxes.

The Gracchi Brothers

The Roman Republic was now victorious and rich, the master of all it surveyed. Its consuls and Senate controlled the fate of nearly all the peoples across the breadth of the Mediterranean Sea. The natural thing to do was to consolidate this power, yet that was not the Roman way. The new warlords were about to make their presence felt.

The first sign of trouble in Rome occurred in 133 BC. Friction was rising between the patricians and plebeians over the distribution of the new wealth pouring into the Republic. Then the tribune Tiberius Sempronius Gracchus made a dramatic proposal. He suggested that stretches of state-owned land in Italy, illegally occupied by the rich, be given to the poor. However, instead of following the standard practice of consulting the Senate, he presented the idea directly to an assembly of the people. Pandemonium erupted, and when a fellow tribune tried to oppose him the latter was hounded from office. Tiberius argued that his populist reforms should be funded by the Republic's newfound wealth from the conquests in the eastern Mediterranean. His new land bill passed, but when he tried to stand for election again he was assassinated by a group of senators.

Next, in 123 BC Tiberius's brother Gaius was elected as a tribune. He realised his brother's weakness was a lack of support at the top of Roman society, and knew the senatorial class would always be opposed to any suggestions that would threaten their own wealth. He therefore cleverly targeted the equestrian and curial aristocracy, securing their backing and then using this support to build a truly populist movement across the Republic. His aim was to carry out a total reorganisation of the Roman state, designed to make it much more balanced in terms of power and wealth. First he avenged his brother by making it illegal for a Roman citizen to be put to death without a trial before the people of the city. He then ensured the law was retrospective which enabled him to target Publius Popillius Laenas who, as consul in 132 BC, had led the investigations into his brother. The latter was forced into exile.

Gaius's most controversial reform however was with regard to the grain supply in Rome. Due to the city's rapid growth it was increasingly reliant on grain imports from Sicily and North Africa. This meant that the price of grain could fluctuate wildly, influenced by factors as diverse as slave revolts, plagues of locusts or simply the size of the annual harvest each year. This fluctuation exposed the citizens of Rome to occasional food shortages when the price was too high or the amount of grain available too low. Gaius therefore stabilised the price of grain at a sustainable level, and introduced a state subsidy to pay for it. To raise the funds for the subsidy he introduced a system of tax farming in Rome's newly conquered territories in the eastern Mediterranean where huge corporations publicly bid for the right to collect the taxes for a percentage of profit. Despite the system being open to huge levels of corruption, which in some cases beggared the new provinces, the people of Rome didn't care. They now had their cheap grain, with the system lasting into the late Republic. It also illustrated the Roman attitude to public administration, with only a small core of officials managing the Republic's vast territory by subcontracting responsibility out to private business and individual *publicani* administrators.

Gaius was now getting into his stride, but realised he would need another term as tribune to complete his reforming ambitions. He didn't want to stand for election himself again, but put forward his closest supporter Fulvius Flaccus to take his place. Such was his popularity that he was re-elected anyway, alongside his friend. Their manifesto was even more radical than that for Gaius's first term of office. It included a plan to enfranchise all Italian citizens, and for a major Roman colony to be built on the site of Carthage, the Punic capital laid waste by Rome at the end of the Third Punic War. Gaius himself travelled to North Africa to see the latter founded. Both policies caused even more friction with the Senate and their supporters, and when Gaius and Flaccus failed to be re-elected in 121 BC they knew they were exposed to retribution. An attempt to drag them before the Senate failed when they refused to attend, Flaccus convincing Gaius that it was a trap, and so it proved. Bloodshed soon followed, with Gaius fleeing and eventually taking his own life with the help of a servant in a sacred grove. Some 250 of his supporters also died, fighting a rearguard action to buy him time to escape, ironically on the same bridge held by Horatio and his companions 400 years earlier.

The Cimbrian War and the Rise of Marius

The next threat to the Republic was external, in the form of the Cimbri. These were a Germanic people who originated from Jutland in modern Denmark. In the 2nd century BC they, along with neighbouring tribes such as the Teutons and Ambrones, migrated south into Gaul where they fought a series of wars with the Gallic tribes there. In 113 BC they invaded the lands of the Taurisci, a confederation of Gallic tribes in Noricum (modern Austria and part of Slovenia). These were Roman allies and the Senate decided to send an army to their aid. The Roman force was commanded by the consul Gnaeus Papirus Carbo who requested the Cimbri retreat. They did so but were deceived by the Romans who set an ambush for them. The Cimbri found out and attacked the Romans first at the battle of Noreia. Carbo's treachery backfired spectacularly with the Romans suffering a huge defeat. They were only saved from complete annihilation by a storm, with Carbo lucky to escape.

This engagement marked the beginning of the Cimbrian War which lasted until 101 BC. The Cimbri could have attacked Italy at this point but chose instead to head west to Gaul where they invaded Roman Provincia in 109 BC. A Roman army under Marcus Junius Silanus was sent to intercept, but yet again the legions were comprehensively defeated. Next, in 107 BC, the Romans were again defeated, this time by the Gallic Tigurini tribe who were allies of the Cimbri. The name of this battle is unrecorded, but shortly afterwards the Romans again engaged the Tigurini, this time at the battle of Burdigala (modern Bordeaux). The result was the same, total defeat, with the consul Lucius Cassius Longinus Ravalla killed.

Much worse was to follow. In 105 BC the Romans resolved to settle matters with the Cimbri once and for all. The new consul Gnaeus Mallius Maximus gathered a huge force of 80,000 legionaries and allies. It was so large that part had to be commanded by Quintus Servilius Caepio, his fellow consul and the governor of Cisalpine Gaul. The two disliked each other intensely so they set off in two separate columns, both arriving at the River Rhône near modern Orange at the same time. Distrusting each other, they camped on opposite sides of the river. Caepio then attacked the nearby Cimbri and their Tueton and Ambrones allies on his own, trying to steal the glory, but his legions were soon crushed. Maximus and his troops saw all this from their camp and became demoralised. When engaged by the Germans they were quickly broken. Many Romans tried to flee but were slaughtered. Altogether the Romans lost 60,000 men, the largest number since Cannae. Only Maximus, Caepio and a few horsemen escaped the engagement, later named the battle of Arausio, with the Rhone choked with dead legionaries for many days afterwards.

Panic now gripped Rome, with the phrase 'terror cimbricus' being used to describe the mood of the people. Roman grit showed through again however, though this time in the form of the great political and military leader Marius. He was born in 157 BC, though not to an aristocratic family. Through sheer hard work and ambition he rose to become a questor in 123 BC, then tribune of the plebs in 119 BC and praetor in 115 BC. Though no great administrator, he proved to be a supreme soldier. His first command was in Spain where he earned fame by defeating a bandit uprising and then setting Rome's silver mining interests there on a firm footing. Then in 109 BC he travelled to Numidia to serve as the *legate* under the consul Quintus Metellus Numidicus. Here the Romans were engaged in the Jugurthine

War against the rogue Numidian king Jugurtha. This had broken out in 112 BC and was proving difficult for Rome to conclude satisfactorily. Marius and Metellus soon fell out, especially when the latter's troops began supporting Marius's own claim to take over complete command of the legions there. Marius then returned to Rome in 107 BC to stand for consul, succeeding and then initiating the reforms of the Roman military detailed in Chapter 1. He was then granted Numidia as his own province where he returned with fresh troops, officially taking control of the campaign from Metellus.

His first act was to send his quaestor and future enemy Sulla to nearby Mauretania to negotiate the kingdom withdrawing its support for Jugurtha. Then, with the help of its king Bocchus 1, Sulla captured Jugurtha and the war ended. Marius was wildly popular among the plebeian classes in Rome and despite Sulla's key role in Jugurtha's demise he was acclaimed the hero of the hour, being granted a triumph where Jugurtha was paraded through the streets of Rome, his royal robes and earrings being ripped off. Thrown into the Tullianum prison, he died of starvation there in 104 BC.

After the shattering defeat of the legions at the battle of Arausio, the Roman people now turned to Marius for salvation. He was elected consul once more in 104 BC, even though he was still in Numidia concluding matters there. Arriving back in Rome for his triumph, he took up his consulship immediately by entering the senate after the victory parade still wearing his triumphator's robes. This didn't impress the conservative Senate, but the people loved it.

Marius now gathered together an army to counter any Cimbri invasion, basing it in southern Gaul. There he waited, training new legions and being elected consul again in 103 BC and 102 BC. In the latter year he finally confronted the Cimbri's allies who had started to move south. At the battle of Aquae Sextiae in Aix-en-Provence he destroyed a combined force of Teutons and Ambrones, inflicting 90,000 casualties on the Germans and capturing 20,000 including the Teuton king, Teutobod.

Marius's newly reformed legions proved to be superior to the Cimbri warriors at the battle of Vercellae, though credit was also given at the time to Sulla who led the Roman and allied cavalry which also played a key role in the battle. Defeat for the Cimbri was total, they lost up to 160,000 men with 60,000 captured including a large number of camp followers. Soon the slave markets of Rome were overflowing.

Marius was elected consul again in 101 BC and in that year was able to tackle the Cimbri head on. The enormous tribe had begun to move south and for the first time penetrated the Alpine passes, entering Cisalpine Gaul. The Roman force there of 20,000 withdrew behind the Po river, allowing the Cimbri to devastate the fertile countryside to its north.

This gave Marius time to arrive with his legions from southern Gaul, totalling 32,000 men, and he led the combined Roman army to an immense victory at the battle of Vercellae near to the confluence of the Po and the Sesia river.

Marius was once again the hero of the hour, though the successful conclusion of the Cimbrian War marked the beginning of the long enmity between Marius and Sulla as the latter felt that, certainly in the Jugurthine War, the consul hadn't given him the credit for his actions. Marius then further alienated himself with the patricians by granting full Roman citizenship to his allied Italian soldiers without asking permission from the Senate. This was to have unforeseen consequences and caused the next great crisis to face the Republic.

The Social War

By now domestic Roman politics was divided between two distinct factions, the *optimates* and the *populares*. The terms, popularised from the later 2nd century BC, referred to the political leanings of their followers. The former were the conservative defenders of the upper classes and the Senate, while the latter advocated reform in favour of the plebeians and popular assemblies. Sulla was the darling of the *optimates*, Marius of the *populares*.

Such disagreements were set aside for a short period in the early 90s BC when Rome was rocked by a conflict that caught many by surprise. This was the Social War, a viscous affair when some of Rome's erstwhile Italian *socii* allies in the Apennines rose in revolt. Troops from the Italian legions, armed in the Roman fashion, had frequently fought alongside Rome's own legions. They had proved so valuable to Marius that, as detailed above, he had granted Roman citizenship to his Italian troops after the battle of Vercellae. However, this gave a newfound sense of power to the Italian political classes who now demanded a greater say in Roman foreign policy. After all, it was their soldiers who were fighting and dying alongside those of Rome. With trouble brewing, in 91 BC the tribune Marcus Livius Drusus proposed new legislation in Rome to try to avert a crisis developing. This would have admitted all Italians to citizenship but provoked a huge backlash in the Senate, with Drusus being assassinated. This was the last straw for the Italians and many now rose in revolt.

The specific peoples who challenged Rome were the Marsi in the northern Apennines and the Samnites, once one of Rome's most feared enemies, to their south.

The two formed their own confederation with its headquarters at the city of Corfinium, due east of Rome across the Apennines. To mark their new alliance they renamed the town Italia and created their own Senate and army. It should be noted that many Italians, for example the Etrurians and Umbrians, didn't join the insurrection.

The rebels were initially successful, the Marsi inflicting defeats on Roman armies in the north and the Samnites bursting onto Campanian coastal plain in the south. There, the rich cities along the Bay of Naples, for example Surrentum, Strabiae, Herculaneum and Nola, fell one by one. Pompeii was spared a siege given it supported the rebellion from early on.

Fine living in the Bay of Naples. The Roman senatorial class of the Republic holidayed together in huge luxury villas there, this example in Oplontis.

Marius was in charge of the Roman forces in the northern sector. Now 67, he was far less energetic than he previously had been and viewed as slower on campaign by the *optimates* than his rival Sulla. The Senate accused him of staying in his military camp in the region for too long, though when he did emerge he inflicted two defeats on the Marsi. He then waited to be appointed supreme commander of all the Roman forces in the field, but when this did not happen he retired to Rome, taking no further part on the war.

The Senate realised this revolt needed to be brought to a halt as quickly as possible and decided to offer the rebels concessions, with the consul Lucius Julius Caesar helping to pass a law which granted Roman citizenship to any Italians who had not participated in the uprising. This may also have extended to those still fighting but who agreed to immediately put down their weapons. The move proved decisive and soon the rebellion began to falter. The Senate then appointed new military commanders tasked with bringing the war to a conclusion. Consul Gnaeus Pompeius Strabo was placed in charge of the three legions in the north, while Sulla was given command of those in the south. Victory followed victory for the Romans, and the war was over by 89 BC.

To cement the peace, more new laws favourable to the Italians were now passed. A key one organised the formal inclusion of all Italians south of the River Po into the Roman state as full citizens, such that from this time all of Italy south of this line was now a single Roman nation. All seemed set for a period of peace after the dramas of the Jugurthine, Cimbrian and Social Wars. However this proved a false hope because, in 88 BC, a full civil war broke out. The protagonists were none other than Rome's two leading warlords, Marius and Sulla.

Civil War

Sulla's First Civil War lasted from 88 BC to 87 BC and occurred in the context of the First Mithridatic War, Rome's first conflict with Mithridates VI of Pontus. This began in 89 BC, with Sulla being given command of the army in his capacity as one of the two consuls. This was a plum command for the ambitious warlord as he knew there was fabulous wealth to be gained from conquering Mithridates's empire in Anatolia, around the Black Sea and in Greece. Some of this territory comprised Roman provinces seized by the Pontic king, so there was also glory to be had restoring Roman rule. However, Marius also wanted the post. Having encountered Mithridates on an earlier tour to the east, when he had warned the king not to fight with Rome, he thought himself to be the expert on the region. Relations between Sulla and Marius, already poor, became increasingly strained and in 88 BC conflict broke out.

The flashpoint occurred when one of the tribunes of the plebs, Sulpicius, suggested that the votes of the recently enfranchised Italians be evenly split among the existing Roman voting tribes. The Senate blocked the move, so he turned to Marius for support, and put forward a long list of proposals to the popular assembly designed to bypass the Senate. One of his suggestions was to take command of the army away from Sulla, the *optimates*'s champion. This was a real threat to the consul and he played for time by retiring to examine the heavens for omens. This was one of his rights as a consul and meant that all public business in Rome had to cease until Sulla had completed his task. Sulpicius now overreacted, bringing his *populares* supporters onto the streets of the capital. Violence between the *optimates* and *populares* ensued, with Sulla having to flee and seek shelter with Marius. The latter saw his opportunity and made a number of demands of the consul who agreed to allow public business to return to normal. In short order he was stripped of his command, with Marius now put in charge of the army to fight Mithridates.

Sulla knew his days would be numbered if he stayed in Rome and fled. He headed south, reaching an army of six veteran legions at Nola in Campania who he had commanded in the Social War. He convinced them to support him before Marius's own tribunes arrived, they then being killed when they tried to take control of the force. The importance of this cannot be underestimated, as it was the first time the legions had chosen to side with a warlord against the Republic itself. Sulla now marched on Rome, joined by his fellow consul Quintus Pompeius Rufus. The pair fought their way into the city and a pitched battle ensued in the Esquiline Forum between the *optimates* and *populares*. There, after a promising start, Marius and Sulpicius suffered a resounding defeat. The latter was betrayed and executed, with Marius fleeing to Africa.

Sulla now took control of the city, posting troops throughout the capital to ensure order. He then addressed the popular assemblies to defend his own actions, before taking away their powers to legislate, unless on a law already passed by the Senate. He then added 300 new members to the chamber to ensure its support. The power of the various public tribunes was also reduced. With peace restored in Rome, at least for now, he sent his army back to Campania and resumed his post as consul.

However, all was not well. Another Roman army was at large in Italy under Gnaeus Pompeius Strabo, the father of Caesar's later rival Pompey. Sulla gave command of the force to his own ally Rufus, but when the latter arrived to take command he was killed by Pompey Strabo's loyal legionnaires. This was only the first of a number of setbacks for Sulla, the most important being the failure of his candidates to replace himself and Rufus as consul for

87 BC. The winners were Lucius Cornelius Cinna and Gnaeus Octavius, the former a well-known opponent of his. To counter this Sulla forced Cinna to vow to support him. However, once in office Cinna immediately broke the oath. He tried to impeach Sulla, but the warlord ignored him. He took command of the army once more and marched east to fight Mithridates.

With Sulla gone Cinna tried to revive Sulpicius's voting plans for the Italians, with his fellow consul Octavius leading the opposition. On the day of the vote the tribunes vetoed the law and rioting ensued in the Forum, with Octavius's supporters chasing Cinna's men away. Cinna fled the pandemonium and headed for Capua in Campania where he won over the loyalty of a Roman force there (Sulla's troops there had already left), additionally recruiting Italians to swell his numbers. The old warrior Marius now returned from Africa to join him and together they besieged Octavius in Rome. The latter secured the backing of Pompey Strabo and his troops, but died soon after helping to repel a Marian assault on the city. Marius then cut off the food supply to the capital.

The armies of the two factions now confronted each other near the Alban Hills south-east of Rome, but before an engagement could occur the Senate turned on Octavius and entered into negotiations with Marius and Cinna. The pair then took control of Rome without a fight, with Octavius beheaded. As a sign of things to come, his head was then displayed in the Forum. A massacre followed of Marius's and Cinna's opponents, with Sulla declared a public enemy. His house was burnt down and property confiscated, his laws repealed, and Marius (for the seventh time) and Cinna became the consuls for 86 BC. It was into this maelstrom of political turmoil that Caesar now came of age, beginning his path along the *cursus honorum* for the first time as the political classes of Rome turned on themselves.

CHAPTER 3

CAESAR'S EARLY LIFE AND CAREER

Julius Caesar was the greatest figure to emerge from the Roman Republic. He had a very keen sense of his own destiny from a young age. In this chapter his family background, childhood and then early political and military career is examined to set the scene for his later dramatic rise and fall.

Caesar's Clan

Caesar belonged to the Julia clan. The Julii were one of Rome's oldest patrician *gentes*, the phrase referring to a group of related families who found common cause on the great issues of the day. They originated in Alba Longa, 19km southeast of Rome. Later in the Republic, when it became fashionable for each clan to associate themselves with a divine origin, the Julii aligned themselves with Iulus, son of Aeneas and founder of the town, claiming him as their clan founder. Additionally, in the origin myths of Rome Aeneas himself claimed to be the son of Venus and Anchises, and the former was an association also embraced by the Julii. Caesar himself used both mythical connections wholeheartedly whenever it provided a political advantage.

The Julii moved to Rome along with many other aristocratic clans after Alba Longa's destruction by Rome under its third king Tullus Hostilius in the mid-7th century BC. The clan are also referenced in epigraphy from an early period at the Alban colony of Bovillae, 11km southeast of Rome.

The Julii were an unremarkable *gentes* for most of its existence before the time of Caesar. Little is known about the 12 clan members who were elected as magistrates in the first two centuries of the Republic, excepting Gaius Julius Iulus who became consul in 489 BC. For some reason the clan wasn't as keen to promote the achievements of its illustrious forebears as were other rival clans, for example the Manlii and Fabrii.

One of the first members to next rise to prominence after Iulus was a Julius Caesar who reached the praetorship during the Second Punic War. He was the first in the family to have the *cognomen* (see below) Caesar, it later being claimed this derived from the Punic word for elephant (*caesai*) after he killed one in battle, though Pliny the Elder later suggested the name derived from a Julii who had been delivered by caesarian section. Given Caesar himself issued coins featuring elephants, he seems to have favoured the martial explanation.

Shortly afterwards the clan split into two distinct lines, each registered to different tribes in the Roman voting census. Caesar's direct family sat within the less successful branch. The next clan member to rise to prominence was Lucius Julius Caesar who reached the consulship in 157 BC. He came from the more successful branch. Next, one Sextus Julius Caesar became consul in 91 BC, while Lucius Julius Caesar became consul in 90 BC, playing a key role in bringing the Social War to an end as detailed above. In the same year the latter's younger brother Gaius Julius Caesar Strabo (the last a nickname meaning 'squinty') became an aedil, a junior public official with responsibilities including public entertainment. Lucius and Gaius were from Caesar's branch of the clan and distant cousins of Caesar's father, though it is unknown from which branch Sextus originated.

The *cursus honorum*:

- *Quaestorship* (lowest ranked magistrate) – 24 years old.
- Tribunate of Plebs/*aedileship* (responsible for public buildings/festivals) – 25/26 years old.
- *Praetorship* (military commander or senior elected magistrate) – 29 years old.
- Consulship – 41 years old. Once at this level the noble could be considered for a Provincial Governorship.

Little is known of Caesar's grandfather, Gaius Julius Caesar, other than his wife's name, Marcia. She was the daughter of Quintus Marcius Rex who had been praetor in 144 BC. The couple had at least two children that we know of, Caesar's father Gaius and a daughter called Julia. Gaius embarked on a public service career from an early age, following the *cursus honorum* set career path for aristocratic Roman men of the senatorial and equestrian classes.

By law there were minimum intervals between holding successive offices, and it was forbidden to repeat an office. However, the rules were frequently ignored, particularly in times of crisis as detailed in Chapter 2. Marius's seven consulships are an outstanding example of this.

Gaius married Aurelia, daughter of either Lucius Aurelius Cotta or his brother Marcus Aurelius Cotta. They came from a leading family of plebian nobles called the Aurelii Cottae. The former was consul in 119 BC, following Aurelia's paternal grandfather who had been consul in 144 BC. Three of her brothers also became consuls, Gaius Aurelius Cotta in 75 BC, Marcus Aurelius Cotta in 74 BC and Lucius Aurelius Cotta in 65 BC.

Gaius's prospects of traversing the *cursus honorum* were certainly boosted by association with the Aurelii Cottae, though it was patronage through his sister's marriage that played the biggest role in his political career. That was because Julia married Marius, the political and military giant of the age. The benefits of this family connection were soon evident, for example Gaius being nominated as one of the ten commissioners tasked with overseeing the settlement of Marius's veterans from the Cimbrian War between 103 and 100 BC. He then became a military tribune before being elected praetor around 92 BC. Next, in 91 BC, he became the governor of the province of Asia in western Anatolia, unusually before he had been a consul. However, his career was dramatically cut short before he could actually stand for consul as in 85 BC he died suddenly, allegedly while putting his shoes on one morning. Thus at the age of 16, Caesar suddenly became the head of his family.

Caesar's Childhood

Caesar was born on 13th July, 100 BC, though some have suggested 102 and 101 BC given the opening sections of Plutarch's and Suetonius's biographies are missing. Both begin when Caesar was in his teens. In his own time his date of birth would have been recorded as the third day before the Ides of Quinctilis in the consulship of Marius and Lucius Valerius Flaccus, in the 654th year after the foundation of Rome.

Caesar was the youngest of the three known children of Gaius and Aurelia. He had two elder sisters, both called Julia, given daughters only received a *praenomen* if the family had several daughters. They were styled Julia Major and Julia Minor when there was a need to distinguish them. Caesar was born in the family home, an important event for senatorial families that tradition demanded be witnessed. Thus, when the birth was imminent, word was sent out to nearby family members and political associates to join the father and wait for the birth in the home. This was to witness that the child was a genuinely new addition to the aristocracy.

In the room where the mother was confined the only male present was a doctor, and even then only if required. Her main attendants were the midwife, female relations and female slaves. Caesar is often associated with having a caesarian section birth, but there is no contemporary evidence for this. At that time such a procedure was only used if the mother was dying in childbirth, and then as a last resort to save the baby. The fact is Caesar's mother Aurelia lived a long life afterwards, even giving him political counsel as he travelled along the *cursus honorum*. Some suggest she actually outlived him, though most believe she died when he was 46. It may be that Caesar's own link with such a birth was through an incorrect identification of him with the ancestor mentioned by Pliny the Elder above. In fact Caesar's birth appears to have been normal in every way, with no mention of any complications such as a breech delivery. These were regarded as bad omens and would have been noted at the time.

Once the baby was born the delivering midwife placed the child on the floor where it was inspected for any abnormalities. This was to assess the child's chances of survival, and also to protect the wider family from ill-favour in the case of defects. The father then had the legal responsibility of deciding whether the child would live or be exposed to die. If the decision was benevolent, fires were lit on the altars in the family home, with the guests who had gathered to witness the birth doing the same in their own homes when they returned. The birth date was then noted, this being an important special occasion for the Romans which was celebrated for the rest of their lives. Then, when a boy was nine days old and a girl eight, a formal ceremony of purification called *lustratio* was performed, designed to rid the child of any evil spirits which had entered him or her during the birthing process. The previous evening a vigil and rites were held which culminated on the day of the ritual with an augury (the observation of flights of birds) and sacrifices. A boy was then

The **tria nomina** comprised the following:

- The *praenomen* or first name, used to identify the individual in informal conversation. It was common for this first name to be used for the first son generation after generation, thus Caesar's father and grandfather were both also called Gaius.
- The *nomen* or main name, the most important as it was the name of the clan to which the individual belonged.
- The *cognomen*, which identified a particular family branch of the clan. Not all members of the upper classes had *cognomina*, examples including Mark Antony and Gnaeus Pompey.

given a *bulla* (special charm), usually made of gold, worn in a leather pouch around his neck. The child, boy or girl, was then officially named. Caesar was named with the full *tria nomina* of the elite Roman upper classes, Gaius Julius Caesar.

As Caesar grew his mother played the leading role in the early years of child care, though like other aristocratic women, Aurelia is unlikely to have breastfed the infant Caesar. This would most likely have been performed by one of the slave women in the household who acted as a wet nurse. She would have been one of a number of female slaves personally chosen by Aurelia to help raise the young child. The mother herself would have performed certain tasks, for example bathing, and Aurelia was later feted as an example of the ideal aristocratic mother.

The stages of a child's life as they grew were important to the Romans. Birthdays were always celebrated, with the festivities including once again the lighting of fires on the household altars, drinking wine, hanging garlands of flowers and eating ritual cakes. Very young children were viewed by the Romans as non-humans given the high rate of infant mortality, but when they reached their first birthday, a stage known as the *anniculus*, they began to gain certain legal rights. The parents could also apply at that stage for Roman citizenship for the child.

At the age of five the *infantia* stage ended, and for the next two years the child was given increasing responsibilities around the home. This was because they were viewed to have more rational minds than previously. Tasks included looking after the household animals, and general chores like gathering materials, though this would have been less the case in aristocratic households where slaves carried out most menial tasks.

At this age children were also differentiated based on gender for the first time, with the social and educational pathways separating. The Romans believed that as children of this age could understand speech they were also eligible for early betrothal. The actual marriage age for girls was as young as 12 though more likely 14, and for men around 25.

At the age of 15 boys underwent a ritual that transitioned them to manhood. This ceremony involved the removal of the *bulla* they had been given at birth, and also the child's tunic. The newly acknowledged man would then, if a member of the appropriate class, put on a toga accompanied by their father and male relatives. A tax was collected by the state from the family at this stage, as it was with a death in the family.

Within the Roman legal system the ages at which a child could have social, moral or criminal responsibility were strictly classified. If they were under the age of 14, the child was deemed to be incapable of criminal intent (*doli incapax*). Nevertheless, once over the age of 10 the child had some responsibility for any criminal act if proven they understood the offense, though with specific penalties based on age rather than adult punishments.

Education was of great importance to the Roman nobility, being managed within the family. Roman aristocrats liked to think their system superior in this regard when compared to the state-controlled education systems of the Greek cities. Primary education for Caesar would have begun at the age of seven. This was at home with a *pedagogue* (private tutor), usually a Greek slave. At this stage he would have learned to do basic mathematics, and to read and write. For the former an abacus was used, while for the latter a wax tablet and stylus. All learning was done by rote. Another focus at this age was on the traditions and rituals of Rome, and the child's family history. Great emphasis was placed on the achievements of his ancestors. The young boy was also introduced to the three personal qualities the Romans valued above all else, *dignitas*, *pietas* and *virtus*. In this way the nobility hoped to install in their children the notion that they as Romans were special when compared to all other peoples. A sense of obligation and duty to Rome thus grew in the child from a young age. This broad home-based primary education for the younger children of the upper classes contrasted with those of the middle classes who sent their children to fee-paying primary schools for a similar, though less focused, education.

After their primary education older boys from the upper classes either went to more advanced schools as *discipuli* (students), usually at the teacher's private home, or continued their education in the own family home. In both settings the more advanced schooling was carried out by a single *magister* or *grammaticus* (schoolmaster) who carried out all of the education. Caesar continued to be taught at home, and we know the name of his tutor. This was Marcus Antonius Gnipho, himself from the Hellenistic east and educated in Alexandria. He had arrived in Caesar's household a slave, but by the time of his education had been freed. This was almost certainly because of the family's satisfaction with his teaching skills for the young men in the household.

The older boys were initially taught the core subjects of Latin and Greek language, mythology and literature. They later moved on to the 'seven liberal arts' of advanced mathematics, music, geometry, astronomy, grammar, logic and rhetoric. With regard to the latter, in 92 BC a law had been passed which banned private schools from teaching rhetoric only in Latin. From that point on such schools, often teaching after the normal schooling hours, were only allowed to teach rhetoric in Greek.

Another focus as the boys grew older was Roman law where they would have learned by heart the Twelve Tables that were the ultimate basis of the Roman legal system.

Physical training for the boys was very rigorous, with young aristocrats taught martial skills, running and swimming on the Campus Martius (the plain of the war god Mars) in Rome where the armies of the early Republic had mustered. They were also taught how to ride a horse, initially bareback. Some of this physical training was carried out by the boy's father, very visibly in public view to show his growing offspring off.

Schooling for the children of the Roman nobility was repetitious, onerous, and prone to regular corporal punishment for the slightest error. In that regard it was common for the families of the children to send a household slave along with the child to ensure no abuse took place if they were educated externally in a school. Boys were taught seven days a week, with no weekend off. No doubt the young Caesar would have been delighted when his schooling ended with his graduation at the age of 15 or 16.

Throughout his childhood years Caesar was raised to think that he was special. Though his clan hadn't the illustrious past of some of his peers, he was the only boy in his family and so knew from an early age that he would inherit the mantle of head of his family without contest. Additionally, his mother Aurelia was highly thought of in Roman high society and this would also have reflected well on the boy.

With his father's untimely death when Caesar was 16, he immediately became the *pater familias* head of the family. He would already have spent a significant amount of time with his father from the age of seven. He would therefore have seen first hand the duties and responsibilities he would inherit later in life, sooner than expected in his case. He witnessed how the nobility greeted and treated each other, would have noted who his father's close political allies were, and was allowed to sit outside the Senate *curia* (meeting place) when his father attended. One can imagine the young Caesar peering into the gloomy interior to see his father take part in the great political debates of the day. He would also have learned who his father's patrons were, and who owed Gaius patronage. A patron was a man of wealth to whom the less wealthy would come to ask for favour, and give loyalty in return. It was a system that allowed much of the political activity of the Republic to be carried out informally, and one Caesar would make much use of later in life.

In the Shadow of Sulla

Caesar's coming of age with the death of his father was well-timed in terms of the opportunities it presented, coming as it did at the height of the civil war between the *optimates* and *populares*. Even though Marius had died on the 13th of January 86 BC at the age of 71, just 17 days into his seventh consulship, in 85 BC the *populares* were still ascendant in Rome. A year later Caesar was surprisingly nominated as the new *Flamen Dialis*, the high priest of Jupiter. The previous incumbent had fallen victim to Marius's purges before his death, a sign of the turbulence Caesar himself would face in the years ahead. The holder of this important post had to be a patrician, and also married to a patrician. This meant Caesar had to break this off his engagement to a girl called Cossutia who he had been betrothed to since a boy, given she came from a plebeian equestrian family.

In short order he was then married to Cornelia, daughter of Cinna. This marked Caesar out as one destined for prominence in *populares* Rome. The wedding was in a rare form called the *confarreatio*, named after the emmer wheat (*far* in Latin) used to make the ceremonial loaf of bread carried ahead of the bride, this eaten later with the groom as part of the ceremony. Ten witnesses were present and, given the seniority of the families, the ceremony itself was meant to be performed by the *Flamen Dialis* and also the *Pontifex Maximus*, the latter the chief high priest of the college of Pontiffs. Together they were the two highest religious positions in Rome, though the former was clearly not present at the wedding given Caesar was the nominee for the vacant post. The wedding was completed with the sacrifice of a sheep, and afterwards the bride and groom greeted the witnesses while sitting veiled on sheepskin-covered seats.

Caesar and his bride then set up home in a rather unfashionable district of Rome called the Subura between the Viminal and Esquiline hills. This was some way from the Forum and the centre of political life in Rome. Most of the houses here were slum tenements, with the Subura having a disreputable reputation, particularly for the prostitution rife there. Living in such an area among the lower classes, one can see the beginning of Caesar's later reputation as a man of the people and champion of the *populares*.

It is unclear if Caesar was officially appointed the *Flamen Dialis*, which would have been a huge early advancement for him on the *cursus honorum*. The post had many benefits, including early entry to the Senate, a great honour for such a young man. However, Caesar would also have been aware that the benefits

Bust of Caesar as a young boy.

of the role came at a cost. That was because the position was for life and would anchor him to Rome given the post's inherent daily duties. He would therefore have no opportunity to govern a province or follow a military career where he might make his name and fortune fighting the enemies of the Republic.

Even if he was officially appointed *Flamen Dialis*, Caesar didn't remain in the post for long because political turmoil soon returned to Rome. After Marius's death, Cinna had continued in office as consul for a while longer. In Greece however Sulla was thriving in his campaign to defeat Mithridates. He had originally landed at Dyrrachium in Illyria in 87 BC with his own loyal legions, there meeting up with Bruttius Sura who was the existing Roman commander in the region. The latter joined forces with Sulla who then met with ambassadors from most of the Greek cities at Chaeronea in Boeotia. Many of these were keen to expel the Pontic forces fighting for Mithridates in the Balkans. The meeting complete, Sulla then targeted Athens which was supporting Mithridates. He quickly besieged the city and its harbour Piraeus, there being joined in his camp by many of his supporters who had fled the Marian purges in Rome, including his own family and a number of leading *optimates*. Sulla also recruited a fleet from Rome's allies in the eastern Mediterranean to ensure there would be no relief force to rescue Athens. Finally, after months besieging the city, his sappers broke in. Athens was sacked and Piraeus burnt to the ground.

In 86 BC Sulla intercepted the main 120,000 strong Pontic army which outnumbered him three to one. At the ensuing battle of Chaeronea he used a clever stratagem, feigning a retreat to draw the Mithridatic army onto hidden palisades built by his legionaries behind which he had mounted artillery. Repeated charges by Pontic scythed chariots failed to break through, as did the Pontic phalanx of Hellenistic pikemen. Sulla then personally helped to repel attacks, against first his left, then right flanks, before ordering a general advance against the tiring Pontic army. Roman victory followed in short order, with many of their opponents slaughtered as they ran away.

Back in Rome Cinna now became concerned by Sulla's success. He therefore sent Marius's consular replacement, Lucius Valerius Flaccus, to take control of the army in the east. However, Sulla knew how to charm his rivals and encouraged Flaccus to join forces with him and mount a two-pronged campaign against Mithridates. He also offered the consul the opportunity to gain the greater glory, suggesting he head north and campaign against Mithridates himself. Flaccus accepted the offer and was soon marching through Macedonia.

Meanwhile Sulla set off to intercept the next Mithridatic force in Boeotia, engaging it at the battle of Orchomenus. Some sources say the Pontic army here was in excess of 150,000, with Sulla again heavily outnumbered. However, he once more used the engineering skills of his legionaries, this time not only digging defensive ditches but also dikes which he used to pen in the huge Pontic army. Theyw then spent two days desperately trying to escape the web of defences built around it, ultimately resorting to a head-on charge at the Roman army. This was drawn up very deep between the dikes, with ditches across its front. The Pontic army made no progress at all and once more was routed, with mass slaughter again as the tired soldiers tried to swim the dikes or cross ditches.

Sulla spent the rest of 86 BC consolidating his position in Greece, using his allied fleet to capture any islands in the Aegean Sea still holding out for Mithridates. Meanwhile Flaccus continued his own campaign against the Pontic king, moving from Macedonia to Anatolia after the final Pontic army in the field fled across the Hellespont. However, at some point late in the year he met his demise at the hands of his *legate* Gaius Flavius Fimbria whom he'd fallen out with. Fimbria now took charge of Flaccus's legions and continued the campaign, the soldiers giving him their loyalty with the riches of Pontus so close at hand.

Early in 85 BC Fimbria targeted the Pontic capital of Pergamum. Mithridates knew he couldn't hold this against the onslaught of legionaries and their allies and fled to the city of

Pitane on the coast to escape by sea. He was able to do this because, unbeknownst to Fimbria, Sulla had been in secret negotiations with Mithridates to quickly bring the war to an end. He knew Cinna back in Rome wouldn't stop at just sending one consul to take over his command, and that he needed to get back to the capital himself to take up the *optimates* cause again. Thus when Fimbria had requested Sulla's *legate* Lucullus bring a squadron to blockade the Pontic king in Pitane, the man refused.

Mithridates now fled to Lesbos, and then on to the city of Dardanus at the southern end of the Hellespont. He knew his position was untenable and so when Sulla offered mild terms he jumped at them, with the Peace of Dardanus being signed there and then. This included handing back all conquered territory to Rome and its allies, giving back any Roman prisoners, providing Sulla with a fleet of 70 provisioned ships and paying 3,000 gold talents in tribute. In return he was granted the title 'Friend of the Roman People' and kept his throne and the original territory of the kingdom of Pontus.

Sulla now moved to tidy things up in the east before heading back to Rome. Top of the list was Fimbria, who he targeted next. Fimbria made matters easy, committing suicide when his troops turned on him at the approach of Sulla. Next he moved to appease his own troops who were unhappy at the lack of plunder after the easy terms given to Mithridates. Sulla allowed them to extort wealth from the Roman provinces in Anatolia and their allies, at least in the short term, telling the locals it was a small price to pay for peace in the region.

It was now 84 BC. Back in Rome, Caesar viewed developments in the east with trepidation given his Marian connections. Cinna was still consul and had raised an army to tackle an insurrection among the tribes of Illyria on the western coast of the Balkans. Some thought this was a means of readying a battle-hardened force against the inevitable return of Sulla. However, he drove his troops too hard and they rebelled against his authoritarian regime, stoning him to death.

His successor was Gaius Marius 'the younger', the son of Marius, who alongside his fellow consul Gnaeus Papirus Carbo renewed the Marian purges against the *optimates*. This was the trigger for Sulla to return to Rome. Short of funds, he left many of his troops in Anatolia but ensured his veteran legionaries were with him. They landed in Italy in 83 BC, and so began Sulla's Second Civil War. Ignoring Rome at first, he campaigned in the north and south to secure the countryside. Then in November 82 BC he approached the capital, aiming to finish off the remaining *populares* leadership once and for all. On arrival he found the gates closed and walls garrisoned with *populares* supporters and their Italian allies. He moved swiftly, assaulting the Colline Gate *(Porta Collina)* where he quickly overcame resistance in a viscous struggle that left many of the defenders dead. The tactics employed here can be seen through analogy with his similar but earlier assault on the Herculaneum Gate at Pompeii at the end of the Social War. Here the archaeological record shows he employed a barrage of ballista bolts and slingshots to clear the walls of defenders, while a testudo of legionaries assaulted and carried the gateway. In Rome, once through the gate his opponents quickly surrendered. He then rapidly seized political control, after which he declared himself dictator. Such a move was not unusual in a time of crisis, when a leading public figure would be given total power to see out an emergency. These powers were normally only for six months, but Sulla ensured there was no time limit on his own appointment. He then turned on the supporters of Marius with a savage vengeance. First he had the seven-time consul's body exhumed and thrown into the River Tiber. Then all statues of Marius were destroyed. Finally he initiated his proscriptions, which saw thousands of political opponents killed or exiled. Rome turned into a bloodbath.

It is at this point Caesar enters his own story for the first time centre stage. This is because two of our key sources, Suetonius and Plutarch, begin their narrative here. Caesar was 18 by this time, and would certainly have been in Rome when Sulla fought his way in and began his bloody purge. This was because of his

Slingshot holes along this wall section of the Herculaneum gate at Pompeii show where Sulla's warriors stormed the town at the end of the Social War.

duties as *Flamen Dialis*, the post for which he was certainly still the nominee even if he hadn't formally been appointed.

Sulla didn't see the Julii as a threat. However Caesar quickly became a target given his wife Cornelia was the daughter of Cinna, and Marius had been his uncle-in-law. In the first instance both Suetonius (*The Twelve Caesars*, Julius Caesar, 1) and Plutarch (*Lives*, Caesar, 1) say that Sulla ordered Caesar to divorce his wife. Here the young man showed great courage, repeatedly refusing while many others in a similar position quickly acquiesced, and this despite increasingly direct warnings from the dictator. We do not know whether Caesar was motivated here by a love for his wife, or by an innate stubbornness not to be bullied, but his actions were undoubtedly brave. This was at the height of the proscriptions when many of Sulla's opponents were disappearing in the middle of the night, never to be seen again.

Sulla now switched his angle of attack on Caesar, targeting his finances. He first stripped away Cornelia's dowry, paying it into the Republican treasury. Next he stripped Caesar of his post as *Flamen Dialis*, whether he had been officially appointed or was just the nominee. Finally, Suetonius adds that Sulla confiscated

Caesar's family inheritance. Soon afterwards the inevitable order was given for his arrest, a sure sign that execution was to follow.

Caesar went on the run, heading into the Sabine Hills in central Italy. He had strong Julii connections there, being moved from friendly house to friendly house every night to avoid detection by the Sullan patrols hot on his trail. Suffering from a bout of malaria, he was finally captured by a legionary patrol while in transit between two locations. However in such troubled times, with questionable loyalties on all sides, Caesar was able to bribe the patrol's centurion Cornelius Phagites to let him go.

Caesar went back into hiding again. He was ultimately saved by the intervention of his mother Aurelia. She convinced the vestal virgins and two of her Aurelii Cottae cousins to plead with Sulla for Caesar's life. The latter were Gaius Aurelius Cotta and Mamercus Aemilius Lepidus, leading Sullan supporters and *optimates* who would both later become consul. The strategy worked better than expected, with Sulla not only relenting but also allowing Caesar to resume his public career. However, Suetonius provides a sting in the tail, having Sulla saying the following while making his pronouncement, 'Very well then, you win! Take him! But never forget that the man you want me to spare will one day prove the ruin of the party (the *optimates*) which you want and I have so long defended. There are many Mariuses in this fellow' (*The Twelve Caesars*, Julius Caesar, 1). While clearly a later-added literary device, this does provide insight into the ambition already being shown by the young Caesar.

He now decided that caution was the best path to take and, fearful Sulla might change his mind, left for Anatolia to join the military. He first served as a *contubernales* (literally, tent companion) aide-de-camp with Marcus Minucius Thermos, the governor of the province of Asia and a leading Sullan supporter. Caesar's role here was to learn his trade as a junior officer, observing the *legates*, centurions and legionaries perform their various tasks on campaign. Opportunity was provided when the city of Mitylene on the island of Lesbos in western Anatolia revolted against Roman rule, no doubt due to the heavy taxation being extracted across the region. It was also suspected of supporting local Cilician pirates who were raiding the sea-lanes along the coast, threatening the regional economy. However, Caesar's activity in the region began with controversy. He was first sent to the court of Nicomedes IV, King of Bithynia and Rome's ally, to request a squadron of warships to support the Roman campaign. He spent so long there that rumours started to spread that he was having an affair with the ageing king rather than concentrating on his duties as a Roman officer. On return to the Roman camp he shrugged the accusations off, going on to serve in the front line with great distinction when Mitylene was stormed. For his bravery he was presented with Rome's highest award for gallantry, the *corona civica* crown of oak leaves. Traditionally this was given when the recipient had saved the life of another Roman citizen. A great honour, Caesar was able to wear the crown both in military parades and also in civilian ceremonies back in Rome.

Caesar next campaigned in Cilicia on the south coast of Anatolia under Publius Servius Vatia Isauricus against the Cilician pirates. However, while fighting there in 78 BC dramatic news reached him. Sulla was dead. The dictator had resigned his dictatorship in 81 BC, restored consular government and then served as consul twice more before retiring from public life to his villa estate at Puteoli on the Gulf of Naples. Caesar now felt secure enough to return home, arriving just as another political crisis began. This was the attempt by one of the existing consuls, Marcus Aemilius Lepidus, to lead a revolt against the reforms of Sulla. Trying to emulate Marius he raised an army and marched on Rome, but was easily defeated. His surviving legionaries, allegedly numbering 53 cohorts, fled to Spain where they joined forces with Quintus Sertorius, the *populares* champion there who was still fighting for the Marian cause.

Caesar was repeatedly offered the opportunity to join Lepidus but shrewdly refused, distancing himself from the attempted coup. He determined the political classes of Rome, whether *populares* or *optimates*, had had enough of continual political turmoil. Instead he tried his hand at a legal career, working as an advocate in Rome's courts. Here those with a legal grievance could approach a lawyer to represent them. His first case was to act for a group of Macedonian noblemen who accused Gnaeus Cornelius Dolabella, their former governor, of extortion. Caesar gave a very good speech at the trial which was well received in Rome, and which he subsequently published. However, his prosecution failed and Dolabella was exonerated and acquitted. He next took a case against the future consul Gaius Antonius who was accused of avarice while serving in the First Mithridatic War. Caesar again lost, though this time because Antonius appealed to the tribune of plebs who vetoed the case, which was then dropped. Although Caesar had again performed well in court, word now reached him that he was making enemies among the nobility of Rome. Once again he decided caution was the best route to take and promptly left the capital for the east. His aim was to study in Rhodes to further improve his rhetorical skills under the renowned rhetorician Apollonius Molon, Cicero's former teacher. That the voyage took place in winter shows the threat to him in the capital was real.

Cilician Pirates

On his way to Rhodes the first truly famous event in Caesar's life occurred, his capture by Cilician pirates near the island of Farmakonisi (Roman *Pharmacussa*) off the cost of southwestern Anatolia. Piracy was endemic in the region, and actually the result of Roman military success there during the past few decades. This was because there was now no major regional power left, other than Rome, to police the littoral zone around the coast and the sea-lanes. As Roman interests here were primarily the extraction of wealth back to the Republican capital, the pirates

Celsus Library in Ephesus. The arches to the right feature inscriptions referencing Caesar.

were left to their own devices. Many of them were actually the former crews who had manned the warships of the Hellenistic navies before their defeat by Rome, and so skilled, professional sailors and marines.

Once in captivity Caesar quickly sent the retainers who had travelled with him to the nearby cities on the Anatolian mainland, for example Miletus, Ephesus, Priene and the religious site at Didyma to raise loans to pay the ransom of 20 talents of silver demanded by the pirates. He passed the time with the only two companions he kept with him, his doctor and a valet. Plutarch indicates Caesar showed bravado here in the face of this very real danger. He says (*Lives*, Caesar, 2):

> He showed such contempt for the Cilicians that whenever he laid down to sleep he would send word to them, ordering them to keep quiet. For thirty-eight days, without a care in the world, he would join in their games and exercises as if they were not his captors but his bodyguard. Writing poems and speeches, he treated them as his audience, and those who did not admire them he called to their faces illiterate barbarians, and would often, as a joke, threaten to hang them.

Suetonius (*The Twelve Caesars*, Julius Caesar, 1) suggests this latter threat was actually crucifixion, and Caesar was as good as his word. Soon the ransom arrived and the 25 year old was released. He headed straight for nearby Miletus where much of the money had been raised. Showing good leadership skills for someone who had never held public office, he convinced the local provincial leadership to help him raise and crew a small fleet. He then headed back to Farmakonisi where he rounded up all of his previous captors. They were sent to Pergamum in chains and imprisoned. Caesar asked for them to be executed. However, the regional governor Marcus Junctus showed no interest as he was in the process of converting Bithynia into a new Roman province following the death of Nicomedes IV. It is likely he actually saw an opportunity to sell the pirates, or even accept a bribe to release them. Caesar would have none of this and promptly headed back to Pergamum where he had the captive pirates crucified. He had clearly developed some respect for them when a captive however, for he had their throats cut before the gruesome procedure began.

The theatre at Ephesus. When Caesar was taken captive by Cilician pirates off south-western Turkey, his friends visited all the key local cities, including Ephesus, to raise his ransom.

After this dramatic interlude Caesar then resumed his journey and headed on to Rhodes where he studied under Apollonius. He was clearly a good pupil as Cicero (see Introduction) and many others thought him the best orator of his day, with a finely tuned use of rhetoric using a simple yet effective style. However, his schooling was cut short by another opportunity for military adventure. This featured Mithridates again who had reneged on his agreement with Rome and sent a raiding party along the coast of Anatolia where it was plundering the territory of Rome's allies. Sensing these might defect to the Pontic king without a show of Roman force, Caesar took a ship to the region and raised a force of local auxiliaries. They engaged the Pontic force which withdrew, and the situation was stabilised. We see here a confident young man, ready to take the initiative when he saw Rome's interests threatened, even when not officially sanctioned.

In late 74 BC or early 73 BC Caesar received another religious appointment in Rome, this time to become one of the 15 pontiffs who served the *Pontifex Maximus*. This was a far less restrictive position than being the *Flamen Dialis* and he immediately returned to the capital, accompanied by two friends and ten

The Temple of Apollo in ancient Didyma, sitting on the peninsula closest to the modern island of Farmakonisi where Caesar was held. His friends gathering his ransom would certainly have visited here.

slaves in a privately chartered boat. Once there he took up his legal career again, before being elected to his first political post as one of the 24 military tribunes in 72 or 71 BC. Given the number of legions in existence by then, such tribunes were much in demand. None of our primary sources say Caesar was deployed to a foreign province at this time, so the likelihood is that he was attached to a military unit in Italy itself. This opens up an interesting possibility as the posting occurred at the height of the famous slave revolt of Spartacus, known as the Third Servile War.

This had begun in 73 BC when the Thracian led a small revolt of gladiators at a training school outside Capua. Not taken seriously enough by Rome, this gradually grew into a serious uprising across Campania which defeated army after army sent to destroy it by the Senate. Spartacus was finally defeated by Crassus, the praetor who had earned a reputation as a ruthless military leader fighting against Marius during the civil wars, at one stage fleeing to Spain and later being the hero of the hour during Sulla's assault on Rome's Colline Gate in 82 BC. Crassus was an equally ruthless businessman, building on his military fame to become the richest man in Rome. Now in charge of the army to defeat Spartacus, he showed the same brutal efficiency. In the first instance, to rebuild discipline in the legions, he ordered a decimation of certain units, whereby one soldier in ten was chosen randomly and beaten to death by his comrades. Martial valor restored, the legions went on to defeat the rebellion in battle, with the 6,000 surviving captives crucified along the Appian Way from Capua to Rome. The signal from Crassus here was clear. Don't challenge the might of Rome.

There is no evidence that Caesar served with Crassus in this campaign, but given he was a military tribune at the time it would seem very likely he played some role in Spartacus's defeat. After that he returned to Rome, where while still in military service he supported a campaign to undo many of the onerous pro-*optimates* laws passed by Sulla, at the same time backing a successful campaign to have his brother-in-law Lucius Cinna returned from exile.

Rome and Spain

Caesar's star was now beginning to rise, attracting the attention of the political classes in Rome. His rhetorical skills and legal expertise were widely acknowledged, and he was an experienced officer and warrior of proven courage. He was now also a father, with Cornelia giving birth to their daughter Julia in the mid-late 70s BC. While Caesar was certainly not a faithful husband, at this point or later in life, his marriage to Cornelia does seem to have been a loving one. Sadly it was brought to an abrupt end in 69 BC when she died after 13 years of marriage, with Caesar giving an oration in her memory which was extraordinary for the time given her young age. It was to be a sad year in terms of family loss for him as earlier in the same year he had given a similar funerary oration for his aunt Julia, widow of Marius, which he delivered from the *rostra* (speaking platform) in the Forum of Rome. This well-known speech, called the '*laudatio Iuliae amitae*', was an opportunity for Caesar to set out his family's high-ranking credentials. He seized on it with both hands, Suetonius (*The Twelve Caesars*, Julius Caesar, 6) having him say:

> The family of my aunt Julia is descended by her mother from the kings and on her father's side is akin to the immortal gods. For the Marcii Reges go back to Ancus Marcius, and the Iulii, the family of which ours is a branch, to Venus. Our stock therefore has at once the sanctity of kings, whose power is supreme among mortal men, and the claim to reverence which attaches to the gods, who hold sway over kings themselves.

Immediately prior to both deaths Caesar began his term as quaestor in early AD 69, a post he had been elected to in AD 70 by the *Comitia Tributa* assembly of the 35 five tribes of Rome. This was later than usual in the normal progression of a career along the *cursus honorum*, but these were far from normal times. It seems likely that many public careers were interrupted by the struggles between Marius, Sulla and their followers, and Caesar was no exception. It is possible that Sulla actually raised the ages of accession to office, and if that were the case then Caesar was certainly a victim of this.

The position of quaestor was the most junior of the formal magisterial posts in Rome and Caesar was quickly attached to the staff of the governor of Hispania Ulterior (Further Spain), Antistius Vetus. This was one of two Spanish provinces formed following Rome's victory in the Second Punic War, it covering much of the west and south of the Iberian peninsular, with neighbouring Hispania Citerior extending along the Mediterranean coast to the Gallic border. However, parts of northern Spain remained unconquered at this time and Hispania Ulterior remained under continual threat from the native Lusitanians there. As in Anatolia, Caesar was immediately presented with an opportunity to display his martial skills. His main role though was to oversee the accounts of the province for the Governor, with whom he got on very well. He performed his responsibilities well, this being noted back in Rome.

Two events occurred during his stay in Hispania Ulterior that were to resonate as his career progressed and have been recorded in detail for posterity. The initial one was his first epileptic fit, a condition that was to dog him for the rest of his life. The second was an encounter with a statue of Alexander the Great while visiting the Temple of Hercules in Cadiz (Roman *Gades*). This reduced him to tears as it reminded him of how little he had accomplished at a similar age. This comparison with the great Macedonian conqueror would drive him on for the rest of his life.

Having served his period of office he returned to Rome in 67 BC, stopping off in Transpadane Gaul on the way. This was the region of the province of Cisalpine Gaul north of the River Po where the inhabitants remained Latin rather than full Roman citizens following the ending of the Social War. Caesar took up the cause of the leading citizens in their campaign for full Roman citizenship, a move that set him in good stead later when recruiting new legions from the region during his Gallic campaigns in the 50s BC.

On arrival in the capital his first move was to remarry, his second wife being a granddaughter of Sulla on her mother's side called Pompeia. Her grandfather on her father's side was another leading *optimates*, Quintus Pompeius who was Sulla's fellow consul in 88 BC. The message here was clear to the political classes of Rome. Caesar had grand ambitions and was willing to set aside, if only for now, his Marian affiliation to continue his progress along the *cursus honorum*. Perhaps because of his late appointment as a *quaestor*, even if common at the time, he knew he had some catching up to do.

Gnaeus Pompey makes his first appearance in Caesar's story at this time too, given Pompeia was distantly related to him. The warlord and later great rival to Caesar, soon to be termed Pompey Magnus (Pompey the Great), was born into senatorial nobility in 106 BC. As with Caesar, his family background was inauspicious, they only achieving their first consulship in 141 BC. After a normal aristocratic childhood he served on the staff of his father Pompeius Strabo who sided with the *populares* during the conflicts between Marius and Sulla. On his father's death however Pompey switched sides, joining Sulla as a free-ranging ally when the latter arrived back in Italy after the First Mithridatic War. He was specifically tasked with recovering Sicily and Africa from the Marians, achieving this in two lightning campaigns in 82 and 81 BC. He developed a hard-man reputation by ruthlessly executing any Marian leaders he captured, even those who surrendered. On his return to Rome he refused to disband his legions, even defying his mentor Sulla who was forced to allow Pompey a triumph through the streets of the capital. He then continued his independent streak by initially supporting the renegade Lepidus after Sulla's retirement, before then turning on him to help crush the rising. Pompey then once more refused to disband his army, bringing pressure on the Senate to allow him proconsular powers in Spain to help defeat the *populares* still active there fighting under Sertorius. He was again successful, though at notable financial cost. In his peace settlement he shrewdly offered reconciliation and rehabilitation to the defeated Marians, looking to the long term when he knew support in Spain would favour his political ambitions. Pompey then returned to Rome where he refused to disband his legions a third time, offering his support in the defeat of Spartacus but in reality using them as a force-in-being to ensure his election to the consulship in 70 BC. With his fellow consul Crassus he then began the unpicking process of Sulla's reforms which, as mentioned above, Caesar supported. Pompey was also accorded a second triumph for his successes in Spain. Then in 67 BC, following a bill by the tribune Aulus Gabinius, he was tasked by the Senate with ridding Anatolia of the endemic Cilician pirate problem which Caesar had earlier fallen foul of. The powers granted to Pompey for this role were unheard of at the time, giving him a vast number of ships and an *imperium* (area of control) stretching out 80km out from the shoreline. He was once again successful, gaining further fame back in Rome. Next, in 66 BC the tribune Gaius Manilius proposed Pompey take over command of the Roman forces fighting Mithridates once again in the Third Mithridatic War, replacing the incumbent Lucius Licinius Lucullus. While the latter had been successful in prosecuting his campaign, he was unpopular with his troops, a key failing for a late Republican warlord. Once in charge Pompey was again victorious, the war concluding with the death of Mithridates in 63 BC.

The Catiline Conspiracy

Back in Rome Caesar supported his new kinsman-in-law Pompey as the latter rose to become the dominant political figure in the capital. Keenly aware of the popularity of the man six years his elder, Caesar had ambitions himself to become a leading politician in his own right. While his wealth would never match the likes of Crassus, he nevertheless used his own money (including much borrowed) to further his own career.

For example, it is at this time that he paid for renovations and improvements to the Appian Way.

Continuing his progression along the *cursus honorum*, in 65 BC Caesar was elected to the post of *curule aedile*, a position that allowed him to stage lavish games in Rome in honour of his father, now 20 years deceased. For this he collected gladiators from all of the best gladiator schools across Italy, with 320 pairs appearing in total, all in silvered armour and with lavish weapons. The Senate became alarmed at this, given the recent revolt of Spartacus, and passed a bill that in future limited the number of gladiators allowed to participate in a given set of games. Nevertheless, Caesar's games were a great success and increased his popularity with the *populares* in particular. With Pompey now away fighting Mithridates, Caesar's star continued to rise in the capital.

Next, in 63 BC he ran for the post of *Pontifex Maximus*, the chief priest of the state religion in Rome. Running against powerful senatorial rivals, Caesar was again successful. This was a spectacular triumph, though his campaign was marred by accusations of bribery on all sides. More drama was to follow as in the same year the consul Cicero exposed the Catiline conspiracy.

Lucius Sergius Catilina was an aristocrat born in 108 BC. He served under Pompey during the Social War, and later gained an infamous reputation as a zealous supporter of Sulla during his proscriptions when he even killed his own brother-in-law. Despite being charged with fornication with a vestal virgin in 73 BC, for which he was acquitted, he progressed along the *cursus honorum* and became a *praetor* in 68 BC. By 66 BC he was the proconsul in Africa, but his bad reputation continued to follow him and a charge of extortion prevented him from standing for consul in either 65 BC or 64 BC. There is then some speculation that, frustrated at some stage during this period, he planned to murder the existing consuls and assume power. Called the 'first Catiline conspiracy', there is little evidence this was true. However later in 64 BC, when Cicero defeated Catiline to be elected consul for the following year, Catiline started to systematically enlist a large body of his supporters with the aim of staging an armed insurrection. Their plan was to seize control of the government. His proposals, once in power, were an extreme form of the *populares* platform, including the proscription of wealthy patricians and cancelling debt. This appealed to a wide variety of discontents, for example on the one hand now destitute Sullan veterans and on the other victims of Sulla's own proscriptions who had been dispossessed of their property.

Cicero, who had a well-established network of spies across Rome, was kept fully up to speed of developments with Catiline's plans. On October 21 63 BC the consul made his move, denouncing Catiline to the Senate in a passionate speech. He charged him with treason and was awarded the 'ultimate decree' by the Senate. This allowed him to enact martial law. Catiline fled Rome on the 8th of November, joining his followers at Faesulae in Etruria, including the veterans who had been organising themselves into an effective fighting force. On the 3rd of December a group of envoys from the Allobroges Gallic tribe arrived in Rome and provided Cicero with evidence they had been approached to support Catiline. This was all Cicero needed to make his final move to extinguish the 'second Catiline conspiracy', he quickly rounding up any of the latter's supporters still left in Rome and executing them. The Senate then dispatched an army under Gaius Antonius Hybrida to destroy Catiline, who moved northeast in an attempt to cross the Apennines. Here he was confronted and, despite fighting bravely against the odds, soundly defeated. Catiline was killed along with most of his supporters,

With the threat of rebellion removed, accusations now began among both *optimates* and *populares* about who had supported Catiline. Caesar himself wasn't immune from the charges, with one of his defeated opponents for the post of *Pontifex Maximus* trying to convince Cicero of his guilt. Fortunately the consul rebuffed the man, with Caesar emerging from the turmoil with his reputation intact.

Caesar was next appointed praetor, before reaching the heady heights of a proconsulship in 62 BC when he was made governor of Hispania Ulterior. He first had to escape the clutches of the increasing number of creditors who were financing his rise to power. Caesar turned to Crassus for help who paid some of his debts and acted as guarantor for others. In return Caesar gave the rich senator his political support against the latter's increasingly overt opponent Pompey. This is the first time we see in Caesar's political career conflict with his later great rival. Caesar quickly left for Spain before his praetorship had ended, even with many debts paid. He was fearful of prosecution while still a private citizen by any remaining unhappy creditors or political opponents and knew once in post he would be immune from legal action for his term of office. This was a pattern he was to follow for the rest of his life, securing increasingly high political office to stay one step ahead of those who would do him political harm.

Caesar once again excelled in his new, more senior position. Mindful of the never-ending threats of raiding into his province he raised 10 new cohorts of legionaries. These were formed into the new *legio* X, which became his own personal legion. At a stroke he had increased the size of the force at his disposal by 50%. He then destroyed two Lusitanian tribes who challenged the authority Rome. The victories were so total that his troops hailed him *imperator*. This was important as it allowed Caesar to formally claim a triumph on his return to Rome.

Back in the capital however his military success resulted in accusations that he'd deliberately provoked the encounters with the Lusitanians to benefit financially.

As the area where he campaigned was one of the poorest in the Iberian Peninsula, he easily refuted this. What is notable here is that his campaigning in Spain at this time showed all of the signs of what was to become his military forte during the later Gallic and Civil Wars, namely swift and decisive action to continually force his opponents onto the back foot, with him leading from the front when necessary. Next, later in the year he reformed the law regarding debt in the province, putting the region on a sound financial footing. Always with an eye on political advancement back in Rome, he then returned the following summer, considering his job in Spain done.

His first task in the capital was of a personal nature, for in 61 BC he divorced Pompeia. Given he had already sided with Crassus against Pompey to obtain the former's financial support, this was a bold move, increasing tensions with the man now dominating political life in Rome. Pompey was about to celebrate his third triumph in the capital following his defeat of both Mithridates and the Cilician pirates. The wealth he'd amassed in the east was enormous, allowing him to pay his legionaries 1,500 denarii each as a bonus, the equivalent of over ten years pay per man. He also claimed to have added the vast figure of 20,000 talents of gold and silver to the Republic's state treasury. This was wealth to rival even Crassus, making him untouchable in Rome's corridors of power. In that context, Caesar's decision to divorce a member of Pompey's family was bold to say the least. This was especially the case in the context of the political history of the capital over the previous 30 years, when political fortunes could change overnight, often fatally.

In reality the reasons for the divorce were purely personal, in the context of the winter 62 BC festival of *Bona Dea* (the 'good goddess'). As the wife of the *Pontifex Maximus*, a post still held by Caesar, Pompeia had hosted this festival along with the Vestal Virgins. Men were not allowed to participate in the event which was associated with fertility, yet a young patrician and ally of Caesar named Publius Clodius Pulcher attended dressed as a woman, allegedly with the aim of seducing Pompeia. He was caught and early the following year tried for sacrilege, this carrying a death sentence if he was found guilty. He was somehow acquitted, with Caesar giving no evidence. Nevertheless he divorced his wife, with Plutarch (*Lives*, Caesar, 9) quoting him as saying 'I thought my wife should be above suspicion.'

Consul

Personal matters taken care of, Caesar next had a difficult choice to make regarding his career. He was now 40 and able to stand for the consulship for 59 BC. Like his father he had already served as a proconsul before looking towards a consulship. This was the wrong way round on the *cursus honorum* aristocratic career pathway, but then again these were unusual times for the Republic. Caesar was well-placed to succeed in his bid for the top magistracy in Rome given he was very popular in the capital, particularly among the *populares*. He also had the money to back an attempt to become consul, through his own wealth and his many loans. Ever mindful of his sense of destiny, while in Spain he had already started writing to the leading men of Rome, particularly the top *optimates* who he knew he would have to win over, hoping to secure their support. Yet he also wanted to celebrate the triumph he was due following his acclamation as *imperator* by the troops in Spain. He could only do this if still serving in the army, yet he could only stand for consul if he laid aside his military post given he wouldn't be allowed to politically campaign in Rome if still under arms. He tried to solve this conundrum by writing to the Senate to ask for permission to be allowed to stand for consul *in absentia* while still in the army. However Cato, the leading *optimates*, vetoed the request. He was already an opponent of Caesar and the two had frequently clashed in the Senate before Caesar had left for Spain, particularly over the Catiline Conspiracy.

Forced to choose, Caesar opted for the consulship and made his bid for power. His rivals for the post in 59 BC were the *populares* candidate Lucius Lucceius and *optimates* candidate Marcus Bibulus. Both were leading politicians of the day. Caesar soon realised that both men would be tough opponents and suggested to the former that they form a pact to bid for office together on a common platform. They made a good team given that, while Lucius had more money, Caesar had the greater influence. An agreement was reached, with Lucius spending a fortune promoting their joint candidacy. The *optimates* found out however and, fearful of Caesar's ambition, similarly promoted Bibulus with their own vast campaigning expenditure. The result was the bribing of nearly all of the leading men of Rome by one side or the other, even the incorruptible Cato taking money from the *optimates* campaign.

The outcome suited neither, with Caesar and Bibulus being jointly elected consul for 59 BC. Fortunately for Caesar, in the electoral system each of the two consuls took precedent over the other on alternate months. Given Caesar won the most votes it was he who was the first to do so in 59 BC. This allowed him to make the first political move. First, he began the Republican year with traditional prayers and sacrifices, a role he was well positioned for given he was still *Pontifex Maximus*. Next he re-introduced the publication of a daily record of the proceedings in the Senate. Then he introduced an item of legislation to the Senate which he hoped would make him the leading politician in Rome, even above Crassus and Pompey. This was the controversial Land Bill, his most populist move to date. This aimed to redistribute publicly owned land to Pompey's veteran troops, and also to many of the urban poor in Rome. It was to be financed by the fabulous wealth Pompey had brought back from the east, and overseen by a board of 20 specially appointed commissioners.

The passing of the legislation through the Senate became a grinding battle of wills between the *optimates*, led by Cato, and the *populares*. However, Caesar was greatly helped by a crucial realignment in Roman politics that had taken place just after his election as consul. This was the formation of the First Triumvirate between the three leading men of Rome. These were the immensely wealthy Crassus, the man of the moment Pompey, and the new arriviste Caesar. The term triumvirate means the board of three, though unlike the later Second Triumvirate between Mark Antony, Octavian and Lepidus, this first was informal in nature. Caesar was already tied to Crassus through the latter's financial support on which he was increasingly relying, which should have nominally set him against Pompey. However, he knew that stability in the capital would only come about through an agreement between Crassus and Pompey, and that the key beneficiary would be himself given it would also reconcile any differences with Pompey following his divorce of Pompeia. Caesar's existing issues with Pompey were exacerbated by he allegedly having slept with his wife while he was away fighting in the east, though given he is also said to have slept with Crassus's wife too, perhaps such activity was viewed as being outside the political sphere.

Negotiations to create the First Triumvirate had begun by letter while Caesar was proconsul in Spain, at the same time as he was writing to the *optimates* to seek their backing to be consul. However, major progress only took place once he had returned to Rome. The deal was sealed once Caesar became consul given it greatly increased his negotiating power. Yet many in Rome were unaware of the development until Caesar started to overtly promote Pompey through the proposed resettlement of his veterans in his Land Bill (Crassus's main benefit was an agreement to limit the investigations into unfair tax collection in the east). By that time things had moved too far for their opponents to separate them. Suetonius (*The Twelve Caesars*, Julius Caesar, 19) says that from this point on the three opposed all legislation that any one of them might disapprove of.

Back in the Senate the progress of the Land Bill became glacial, with Caesar's fellow consul Bibulus taking a leading role alongside Cato. He vetoed a key stage of the legislation and then tried to have the remaining days allotted for its discussion declared public holidays, effectively timing it out. However, Caesar now called upon the support of his fellow triumvirs. The following day he reintroduced the bill in the Senate, with Plutarch (*Lives*, Caesar, 14) saying that both Crassus and Pompey now stood either side of him. Further, a force of Pompey's veterans surrounded the debating chamber. When the three tribunes present tried to veto the bill again, Pompey put his hand on his sword pommel and announced that if they did that, violence would ensue. The bill unsurprisingly passed, with Bibulus having a bucket of excrement thrown over him as he left, he then retiring from public life for the remaining period of his consulship, refusing to leave his house.

With the humiliation of Cato, Bibulus and the *optimates*, Caesar was now ascendant and ruled as a lone consul. Suetonius (*The Twelve Caesars*, Julius Caesar, 20) says a popular joke in Rome described the consuls for the year 59 BC as Julius and Caesar, rather than Caesar and Bibulus. However, the *optimates* continued to mount a political guerrilla war against the consul, with Cato at one stage being ejected from the Senate and imprisoned, while another opponent named Lucius Lucullus was so frightened by Caesar's legal threats against him that he is said to have fallen to his knees to beg the consul's forgiveness. Caesar was getting a taste for power, and was master of all he surveyed, at least for his year as consul.

Next he married again, this time to Calpurnia, the daughter of Lucius Piso who by that time had been elected to replace him as consul the following year. Born in 75 BC, Calpurnia was described by contemporaries as both humble and pious, maybe even shy. The marriage resulted in no children and seems to have been another political union. Around the same time Caesar's daughter Julia from his first marriage also married, to his new ally Pompey, further cementing the relationship between the two triumvirs.

Caesar now looked to his fortunes beyond his year as consul. He knew that once out of office he would be targeted by the *optimates*, especially in court where his record as consul would be challenged by Cato and others. His solution was to once more take an office that would make him immune from prosecution, namely another proconsulship. When he had first been elected consul, but before he had taken up his office, the *optimates* had tried to limit his future power by allocating him responsibility for the pastures and woods in Italy rather than allowing him to bid for another proconsulship abroad. However, once in power and with the help of Crassus and Pompey, Caesar had this overturned and instead had himself appointed proconsul in Cisalpine Gaul and also Illyricum (the north eastern Balkans, very much the junior province of the two in terms of what followed). He later added Provincia in southern Gaul to his Gallic responsibilities after the death of its governor. The Gallic territories gave him the four legions mentioned in Chapter 1, including his own founding, *legio* X which had moved north from Hispania Ulterior. Caesar also set the term for his new governorships at five years from 58 BC, making him immune from prosecution once in position through to 53 BC. This proved a shrewd move as, once his consulship officially ended and he could take up his new post, he narrowly avoided an immediate prosecution for legal and financial irregularities when consul. Never one to lose the initiative, he quickly left for Cisalpine Gaul to take up his proconsulship there. This set the scene for the two events which were to define the living Caesar more than any other, namely his campaigns in Gaul through to 52 BC and the later vicious civil war against Pompey which turned into a death match for ultimate power across the Republic's growing *imperium*.

CHAPTER 4

CAESAR IN GAUL

Caesar believed himself a man feted to be the leading political and military figure of his day, with a sense of destiny that knew no bounds. He was now at the top of the political ladder in Rome, though keenly aware that his opponents there were forever snapping at his heels, waiting for an opportunity to bring him down. Yet his greatest glories were still ahead of him, as well as his final, dramatic denouement. This chapter considers his first taste of true glory, with his eight-year conquest of Gaul.

The Helvetti

When Caesar set out from Rome for his new province in Gaul he was 41, and deeply in debt. He knew there was money to be made from being a provincial governor, even if he hadn't made much while in Hispania Ulterior. There was even more to be made through conquering enemy territory, as Pompey had found in Asia. With that in mind, Caesar already had his eyes on the Gallic territories north of the Alps and Provincia. Such conquest would have granted him something else too, namely glory. He was still to have a triumph in Rome, having turned one down to stand for consul. Surely there would be opportunity here, in the

Alexander the Great defeated Darius III at Gaugmela. Caesar wept when he saw a statue of his in Cadiz, lamenting that he had not matched his accomplishments at the age the Macedonian king died.

untamed lands of Gaul, at least as the Romans would have seen it. Back in Cadiz he had looked upon the statue of Alexander the Great and felt inferior. He was now playing catch up.

Looking to his north, Caesar would have seen five broad tribal groupings in Gaul and beyond. These were Gallia Aquitania in the southwest, Armorica in the west, Gallia Celtica in central Gaul, Gallia Belgica to its north, and then Germania across the River Rhine. The most southerly tribes were already coming under Roman cultural influence by this time, with wine a particularly sought after import for the Gallic nobility. Roman merchants were well-embedded in the region, with the River Rhone providing a ready means of accessing central Gaul and the lands north of the Alps. A relative peace had settled across Gaul after the Cimbrian War at the end of the last century, though this was shattered in 63 BC when the Aedui tribe in Gallia Celtica were heavily defeated by their Sequani and Averni neighbours, helped by German allies, at the battle of Magetobriga. The Aeudi were Roman allies, providing a buffer between Provincia and the Gallic lands to the north, and the Romans would have noted the conflict with some alarm. However, it was the Helvetti in the south east of Gallia Celtica who were the first to attract the attention of Caesar.

The Helvetti were a confederation of five interrelated tribes living on the Swiss plateau, surrounded by the Alps and the Rhone and Rhine rivers. By the time of Caesar's appointment in Gaul they were coming under increasing pressure from German tribes expanding from the north and east, and began planning a mass migration west. Caesar (*The Conquest of Gaul*, II, 1) describes the confederation as very warlike, and frustrated that the geography of their location prevented them from carrying out the raiding common among the Gallic tribes.

Led by the Helvetti warlord Orgetorix, the confederation sent word to their neighbouring tribes about their forthcoming migration, asking for safe passage through their territories. An alliance was secured with the Sequani warlord Casticus to their north and the Aedui warlord Dumnorix to their west. Caesar himself (*The Conquest of Gaul*, II, 1) says the three leaders planned to ultimately become the masters of all Gaul, and when Orgetorix's plan was found out by his own Helvetti he was put on trial, later escaping and killing himself.

The Helvetti spent two years planning their migration, gathering cattle from far and wide and stockpiling grain. When word of this reached Rome in 60 BC the Senate sent a delegation north of the Alps to meet the Helvetti leadership. This diplomatic outreach seems to have been successful as the Senate felt conflict with the Helvetti had been averted. Nevertheless planning continued for the migration, and despite the setback with Orgetorix's untimely demise, once ready the confederation set off westwards. This was a massive population shift, with 368,000 migrants on the move, including 92,000 warriors. As they departed their homelands they burned all of their towns and villages to ensure there was no going back, and to deny them to any enemies moving in to occupy their former territory.

For once Caesar here seems to have been caught by surprise. When word reached him of the Helvetii migration he was in Provincia where he only had one of his four legions with him. This was likely *legio* X given its recent transfer from Hispania Ulterior. It would have been immediately apparent that the sheer scale of the Helvetii migration would significantly disrupt Roman trade routes through Gaul and destabilise Provincia. This was just the opportunity Caesar needed to start campaigning north of Roman territory and he quickly seized it. Heading north with his legion and some rapidly recruited allies from the native Gauls, he soon reached the Rhone ahead of the Helvetti where he burned the only substantial bridge across the river. He then arrayed his troops along the western bank as a blocking force. As the Helvetti approached the broad river they realised their path was blocked and sent a delegation to meet Caesar. He stalled them on the far side of the river for 15 days, using the time to fortify his position with a ditch, rampart and palisade 30km long. Then, when he felt secure enough to defend the line of the river in the event of a full assault, he finally allowed the delegation of Helvetti nobles across to meet him. They asked for permission to pass peacefully through Provincia, saying their ultimate goal was Gallia Aquitania on the Bay of Biscay. Caesar refused, saying any attempt to cross would be met with force. The delegation returned empty handed, much to the frustration of the mass of migrants who by this time were hard pressed to feed and water themselves. For such a huge mass of people on the move, continual momentum was everything. Soon small groups tried to cross the river but were easily beaten back by the Romans behind their fortifications, with ballista, bowmen and slingers preventing all but the most hardy from reaching the western shore. Caesar's legionaries quickly dispatched these, reminding his troops of the savage defeats inflicted on the Romans in the region by the Germanic Cimbri and their allies 40 years earlier. The message here was simple. The Gauls and Germans were not to be trusted.

The Helvetti leadership, probably unaware that Caesar only had the one legion plus his allies with him, now looked to travel around the Roman fortifications. They engaged with the Sequani and the Aedui again to ask for permission to head northwest before turning south. Caesar was now aware of the full strength of the Helvetti and knew he wouldn't be able to stop the migration with the troops to hand if he was challenged again, so he left the legion in place under his *legate* Titus Labienus and left for Cisalpine Gaul. There he gathered the three incumbent legions, VII, VIII and IX, and recruited two more from the Italicised Gauls there, calling them *legios* XI and XII. He then headed back north with the whole force, this numbering at least 27,500 legionaries together with 4,000 allied Gallic cavalry and some light troops. He crossed the Alps, sending word to his Aeduian allies to stockpile provisions ready to supply his army when they arrived in the campaigning theatre. His column fought a number of skirmishes with small, hostile tribes as they traversed the mountains, before eventually arriving in the rear of the Helvetti column.

The migrants had by this time already moved through the Pas de l'Ecluse between the Rhone and the Jura mountains, and through lands of the Sequani, and were now skirting the territory of the Aedui and their Ambarri and Allobroges neighbours. Given the size of the Helvetti force they had no choice but to plunder the land they now passed through for provisions and the suffering Gallic tribes now sent embassies to Caesar to ask for direct help. He was hot on the heels of the Helvetti column and eventually caught up with it at the Saône river, a right hand tributary of the Rhone. Three quarters of the Helvetti had already crossed, using rafts and small boats, but a Helvetian clan called the Tigurini were still waiting on the shore for their turn to cross. This was the tribe who, allied to the Cimbri, had defeated a Roman army in 107 BC. Caesar was aware that the grandfather of his father-in-law, the consul Calpurnius Piso, had been killed in that battle. He lost no time in extracting a brutal vengeance, swiftly deploying his legions into three lines and advancing in a surprise attack that pinned the Gauls against the river. In the ensuing battle of Arar the Tigurini were shattered, the survivors fleeing into nearby woods where they were hunted down by Caesar's allied cavalry.

Seeing their kinsmen slaughtered, the remaining Helvetti headed off again. Caesar's pursuit was unrelenting, he building a wooden military bridge across the Saône and crossing his whole force in a single day. This utter ruthlessness to bring his enemy to battle set the tone for the remainder of Caesar's military actions across Gaul over the next eight years, never letting his opponent settle once in the field. The Helvetti realised they were unable to shake their pursuer and halted to send another delegation to Caesar. This was led by one Divico, a very elderly man given he was one of the war leaders who had beaten the Romans in 107 BC. The Helvetti offered to settle wherever Caesar suggested in return for peace with Rome, though adding that they still believed they would win any military engagement if the Romans forced a battle. Perhaps the Gallic victory in 107 BC was mentioned again, this clearly the reason Divicio had been chosen to lead the Gallic mission. Caesar was having none of this, warning the Helvetti not to be overconfident and saying he would only agree terms if they agreed to provide hostages. He also demanded they pay reparations to the Aedui and their neighbours. The Gallic delegation recoiled at this and stormed off.

The prospect of a peaceful solution all but over, the Helvetti set off yet again, now heading south west towards Gallia Aquitania. Caesar followed close on their heels, his cavalry snapping at the rear of the Gallic column. However, on one occasion they over extended themselves and were ambushed by 500 Helvetti cavalry who routed them, Dumnorix and his Aedui fleeing first. This emboldened the Helvetti whose rear guard now began to offer battle whenever the Romans approached. Caesar refused to engage at this point, keen to steer the Helvetti away from Aeduian territory before committing to a major battle. Instead he stayed close enough to prevent the migrants from raiding the surrounding countryside, always staying within 8km of his opponents.

The Helvetti column was now well away from the Saône and Rhône, which Caesar had been able to use to supply his force by barge, and the Roman pursuers began to run out of provisions. Supplies promised by the Aedui failed to arrive despite constant Roman requests, it then transpiring that Dumnorix was leading a group of nobles who favoured an alliance with the Helvetii rather than side with the Romans. They deliberately held up the Roman provisions. Caesar found out and acted quickly, summoning the warlord and confronting him. Dumnorix admitted his guilt and for once Caesar was merciful, deciding to give him another chance rather than executing him. However, the Aedui chieftain was under constant observation from that point onwards. Meanwhile Aeduian supplies now resumed to the Romans.

Caesar still had the short-term problem that his troops were short of supplies until the provisions from the Aedui built up again. He therefore decided to try and bring the campaign to a swift resolution and decided to attack to the Helvetti. For this he devised a clever stratagem whereby he split his force into two, with two legions being sent out very early in the morning, two hours before Caesar led out the rest of his troops, he now having in total six legions given they had been joined by *legio* X. The two legions departing early were given orders to position themselves out of sight above the Helvetti camp, only to attack when they saw Caesar's legions arrive. It was a clever plan but failed because the two Roman forces lost contact with each other, one of Caesar's officers misreporting that the first Roman force was actually Gallic. The Helvetti, unaware they had narrowly avoided battle, now broke camp and set off westwards again, though this time Caesar didn't pursue given his worries over supplies. He headed back to the nearby Aeduian town of Bibracte, hoping to get provisions there. However some of his Gallic allies promptly deserted and told the Helvetti of Caesar's plight. Soon the hunter became the hunted as the Helvetii reversed their course to pursue the Romans.

Whether intentional or not, Caesar now knew he would have his battle and chose a steep hillside on one side of a valley for the engagement. He drew up *legio's* VII, VIII, IX and X in the usual three lines, with his cavalry and light troops on their flanks. However he held back the raw *legios* XI and XII at the top of the hill, hoping not to have to use them given their lack of experience against an enemy with at least three times the Roman strength.

In the ensuing battle of Bibracte the Helvetti charged headlong uphill into the Roman legionaries. These threw their lighter *pila* as the Gauls broke into their charge, holding back the heavy *pila* until the Helvetti were at point blank range. Then they drew their *gladius*, set their *scutum* shields and took the weight of their opponent's charge before countering with swift, brutal thrusts of the *gladius* into the Gauls' exposed midriffs. The Romans were soon on top, pushing the Helvetti back down the hill despite the weight of numbers. All seemed to be going well until 15,000 more Boii and Tulingi allies of the Helvetti suddenly appeared on the Roman right. These were likely arriving from further back in the Helvetti column rather being a clever ploy given the limitations of Gallic command and control on the battlefield. Caesar had no such problems and quickly re-deployed his third line to counter the new threat. This contained, he then continued his assault on the Helvetti centre, pushing them back to their wagon laager on the other side of the valley. That the XI and XII legions were not deployed at any time in the battle indicates that Caesar was never worried about its outcome, even though the fighting continued until after nightfall. The fighting was most brutal around and within the Helvetti laager, but eventually the Roman victory was complete though with heavy losses.

The defeated Helvetii now offered their surrender which Caesar readily accepted. Some 6,000 from the Verbigeni tribe avoided capture and fled north, they later being captured by Caesar's Gallic allies and returned to the Romans. He executed every man, woman and child to send a sharp message to the remaining Helvetti. These he then resettled back in their homeland with orders to rebuild it, giving them the supplies to feed themselves while they did so. Given only 110,000 made it back, the Helvetti confederation paid a terrible price for their migratory adventure. Meanwhile, it was at this point that Caesar first sat down with his scribes to draft his first missive regarding his exploits to send back to Rome. He had been victorious, and wanted the world to know about it.

The Suebi

Caesar was now positioned in Gallia Centrica with six legions. He had tasted victory and wanted more. His first thought was to move southeast to his province of Illyricum in the western Balkans. Though there was still time left in the campaigning season, he decided this would be too far. He therefore looked to Gaul again, where the natives presented him with his next opportunity.

When word reached the various tribes of Gallia Centrica and further afield of Caesar's decisive defeat over the Helvetti, many sent delegations to congratulate him. The envoys asked for permission to call a gathering of tribal chieftains to meet with Caesar and present him with petitions. When this meeting took place a number from eastern Gauls tearfully begged Caesar to intervene against a German tribal confederation called the Suebi. This was because earlier the Sequani had asked for help from their German neighbours across the Moselle in a border dispute with another Gallic tribe. Once resolved however, the Suebi had then refused to return home. Some 120,000 were now camped in eastern Gaul where they were exacting tribute and taking hostages from all of the regional tribes.

The Suebi, led by their king Ariovistus, comprised a large number of Germanic tribes including those later called the Marcomanni, Quadi, Hermunduri, Semnones and Lombards. They had a reputation as fierce warriors. Caesar saw here another opportunity to show his martial prowess and quickly agreed to help the Gauls. In the first instance he sent word to Ariovistus that he wanted to meet with him to discuss the situation, suggesting they gather halfway between their two locations. The German king declined, also asking why the Romans felt they could intervene in events in this part of Gaul, way to the north of Cisalpine Gaul and Provincia. Caesar then sent another message, this time with clear instructions for Ariovistus. This included not bringing any more Germans into Gaul, refraining from any further raiding and returning the Gallic hostages to their tribes. He threatened to use force if his demands were not met. Unsurprisingly, Ariovistus refused again, with the Germans raiding the territory of the Aedui to reinforce the message. Caesar also received word that thousands more Suebi were now massing further east, waiting to cross the Rhine and Moselle to join the Germans already in Gaul. He decided to act immediately, securing his grain supply and then marching his whole force eastwards at a rapid pace. The Suebi countered by moving on the Sequani capital of Besançon (Roman *Vesontio*), prompting Caesar to move even more quickly in a series of day and night marches. He arrived there first and installed a garrison before allowing the troops a few days rest.

While in Besançon Caesar had to face down some serious discontent amongst the officers of some of the legions who were worried about campaigning so far from their home territories. They were particularly worried by the rough terrain they were likely to have to pass through as they pressed their offensive, where they felt they would be vulnerable to ambush. Here Caesar again displayed his skills in leadership and rhetoric, threatening to take only the Xth legion with him. The tactic worked, shaming the others into following, and the following day the whole column moved out. However Caesar did ensure that they took a longer route that avoided most of the difficult terrain. He had listened to the concerns of his men.

Within a week Caesar's allied cavalry had found the huge German army. Once Ariovistus was aware of his nearby opponent he again reached out, this time agreeing to a meeting with

Caesar. He insisted however that both parties, when meeting, only brought mounted warriors with them. Caesar didn't trust the Gallic horse in his army for this delicate encounter. It was here therefore that he mounted as many of the Xth legion as possible on the Gallic horses, hence the legions name from this point being *legio* X *Equestris*.

This meeting again failed to break the impasse, the Germans initially threatening the Romans though adding they would support them in the future if Caesar withdrew. He rebuffed them however, declaring he would remain where he was. Some of the German cavalry with Ariovistus then started throwing javelins and stones at Caesar's legionaries and the meeting broke up with the Romans withdrawing to their camp in good order. Caesar did well here to prevent his troops from responding to this provocation, clearly a trap. His instincts were proved correct two days later when he sent two envoys to the German camp at the invitation of Ariovistus, the German leader promptly throwing them in chains.

Battle was now inevitable. Having learned from his Helvetti campaign, Caesar first made sure his lines of supply were secure given the distance from Roman territory. To do this he marched his force towards the German camp, deploying into the usual three lines when within sight of it but using the last line to actually build a large marching camp covering one of main supply routes from central Gaul. While the legionaries finished the camp those in the first two lines fought off any German attempts to disrupt the on-going construction. Once finished Caesar then garrisoned the new camp before leading his remaining troops back to the original camp. With two well-fortified camps protecting his lines of supply and troops, he now had freedom of manoeuvre without worrying if his provisions would arrive.

The next day Caesar again deployed his army in three lines ready for battle, but the Germans declined and so he again returned to his camps. A desultory German attack on the new camp was then easily beaten back. Caesar now found out that the Germans were avoiding a battle because their diviners had told Ariovistus that he would only win an engagement if there was a full moon. Caesar decided to act immediately to wrong foot the Germans and play on their superstitions. The next day he deployed his whole force again, including those troops who had been guarding the camps, into the usual three lines. He then advanced them as close to the German camp as possible where he knew Ariovistus would have to engage or lose face. The German leader chose the former and his army deployed into a line of battle based on clan and tribe, each led by their own individual leaders.

This huge engagement is known as the battle of Vosges and began with a sudden charge by the Germans. The Roman first line held, as usual the legionaries throwing their lighter *pila* at longer range and the heavier one at point blank range before drawing their *gladius* and setting their *scutums*. They then began to slowly push back the German left wing where Caesar had taken personal command of his Xth legion. At one stage the Roman left itself was threatened by weight of German numbers, but the prompt action of a cavalry commander saved the day. Finally, Caesar broke through the German line on their left and then turned inwards towards their centre. This promptly broke. Soon the whole Suebi army was in flight, with Caesar now taking charge of the pursuing cavalry. No quarter was given and the German army was massacred, with Ariovistus being one of the few to escape, only to disappear from history. The result was total victory for the Romans, with the additional Suebi waiting to cross the Rhine and Moselle now returning home.

Caesar was well-satisfied, boasting he had '…completed two important campaigns in a single summer' (*Conquest of Gaul*, II, 2). He again called his scribes and narrated his exploits as a new set of commentaries, which he then sent to Rome once more. He then put his six legions into winter quarters in the territory of the Sequani and headed back to Cisalpine Gaul. There he fulfilled his normal administrative role as proconsul, while planning his next set of campaigns for 57 BC. However, his new target was to be a far more ambitious challenge than the Helvetti and even the Suebe, namely the Belgae in the far north of Gaul.

The Belgae

While in Cisalpine Gaul over the winter of 58 and 57 BC Caesar recruited two more legions, the XIII *Gemina* and XIV. He used the experienced centurions from his six other legions to form their officer corps, with seasoned legionaries similarly becoming their new centurions.

Over the winter Caesar received reports suggesting that the Belgae tribes in Gallia Belgica in the far north of Gaul were conspiring against Roman interests in Gallia Centrica. They feared, quite rightly, that soon they would become the subject of Caesar's attention. Roman concerns were confirmed when an allied Gallic tribe was attacked by an unnamed Belgae tribe, with Caesar immediately sending word to his Gallic allies that he was on his way to deal with the situation. He then headed north with his two new legions, joining the existing six in the lands of the Sequani and then targeting the nearest Belgae tribe in the north, the Remi. His reputation preceded him and they immediately sent envoys, declaring their peaceful intent and offering hostages and supplies. Caesar also asked them for details of the numbers of warriors the various other Belgae tribes would field in battle if it came to war and here we have the very precise figures they provided:

•	Bellovaci	60,000
•	Suessiones	50,000
•	Nervii	50,000
•	Morini	25,000
•	Atuatuci	19,000
•	Atrebates	15,000
•	Ambiani	10,000
•	Caleti	10,000

A further six unspecified Belgae tribes together agreed to provide 50,000 more warriors, giving an enormous overall total force of 289,000 warriors.

Caesar was unperturbed. He ordered a general advance and the Romans soon found themselves marching through the land of the Nervii. After three days they learned that this Belgae tribe and its allies were massing on the far side of the River Sambre (then known as the Sabis), ready to pounce on his column. Further intelligence uncovered the Belgae plan that aimed to separate the lead legion and its baggage train from the rest of the Roman force and annihilate it before the whole Roman force could deploy. Caesar therefore redeployed his column such that all of his legions were in mutually supporting positions.

When he reached the river Caesar began building the usual marching camp to protect his force overnight. His scouts reported the Nervii were hidden in wooded terrain on the opposite bank, and that the river, while wide, was only 1m deep. He therefore ordered his allied cavalry and light troops to ford across to close on the Nervii and scout their positions. A general skirmish then developed, with the Belgae horse trying to keep the Romans away from their own hidden foot.

The Nervii, seeing the legions deployed to prevent their separating one from the others, now chose to engage en mass and the entire army charged from their hiding places, routing the Roman cavalry and light troops and storming across the river. Here they hoped to catch the Romans before the marching camp had been built. So began the battle of the Sabis, where the speed of the Belgae attack almost caught the Roman legionaries out. Many were still out of their armour, with their weapons set down while going about their construction task for the marching camp. Caesar had prepared for this however, having ensured the legionary commanders had all stayed with their units in case they needed to move quickly. They now did so, Caesar giving the order to form into battle formation. The Romans just managed to do this before the ferocious Nervii charge hit them. Nevertheless, many Romans had to fight the battle without helmets and with their shields still in covers given they had no time to properly equip themselves.

Caesar once more based himself with the Xth legion on the left wing and again fought with great bravery, leading from the front when necessary and repeatedly moving to where the fighting was fiercest. When he judged that the Nervii charge had run out of momentum there he ordered the Xth and IXth legions to charge the disrupted Gauls. This shattered their right flank, which the Romans drove back over the river. Once there the two legions then withstood a counter-attack by the Atrebates allies of the Nervii, which was also routed. Meanwhile, in the centre *legios* VIII and XI now pushed their opponents back over the river to join Caesar and his two legions.

With victory in sight, Caesar was now presented with a crisis. The advance of the four legions on his left and in the centre had opened a gap with the Roman right wing that was seen by the Nervii. They formed a column that stormed through it to attack the Roman camp and encircle the two legions on the Roman right. The camp defenders, which by this time included the now rallied cavalry and light troops, promptly bolted, leaving the legionaries on the Roman right to their fate. These were so crammed in by the Belgae attack that they couldn't use their weapons effectively. In particular *legio* XII was suffering, with every centurion in its fourth cohort dead and its standard bearer down and the standard missing. Many centurions in the legion's other cohorts were also killed or wounded.

Caesar assessed the situation and acted quickly. He ordered the four legions with him to continue to press forward to keep pressure on the Belgae. He then crossed back over the river and joined the XIIth legion. There he seized a shield and fought in the front line again, calling on the remaining centurions by name and restoring first morale and then order. He next ordered the neighbouring *legio* VII to deploy to the rear of *legio* XII so that they fought back to back. Gradually the Roman right stabilised.

Word now reached him that the Xth legion had seized the Nervii camp and he deployed his reserve, the new *legios* XIII

Gemina and XIV. This enveloped the remaining Gauls fighting the VIIth and XIIth legions and the Nervii broke, being pursued back across the river. At this point the cavalry and light troops returned, sensing the spoils of victory, to harass the fleeing Gauls. Caesar even deployed light ballista in the pursuit. Here and there pockets of Nervii put up a dogged last stand, only to be massacred. Finally the battle was over with another great Roman victory. Caesar had again showed great leadership and martial skills, with his reputation as a great warlord further enhanced not just with his own troops but with his enemies too. Belgae resistance to the Roman advance was broken, with all but one of the remaining tribes now submitting to Caesar. This was the Atuatuci who occupied a single fortified town on a hilltop that they felt they could easily defend. Caesar circumvallated the settlement with a ditch and rampart, along the length of which he built a number of small forts in which he mounted artillery. He then began building siege towers, and ramps to allow them to approach the hilltop walls. This was the first time the defenders had seen such tactics and technology and, overawed, they eventually surrendered. However, at some stage they reneged and attacked the Romans who then defeated them easily. Caesar decided to make an example of the tribe to deter any further Belgae insurrection and placed the entire remaining population of 53,000 into slavery. Such was the price paid for challenging Caesar, who was now effectively master of all Gaul.

The Conference of Lucca

After the end of another fruitful campaigning season Caesar again returned to Cisalpine Gaul. There his thoughts turned to Rome where the triumvirate with Crassus and Pompey was being increasingly criticised in a campaign led by the *populares* champion Publius Clodius Pulcher. This was the same man whose alleged attempt to seduce Pompeia during the 62 BC festival of *Bona Dea* had led to Caesar divorcing his wife. Caesar also knew that both of his fellow triumvirs were increasingly uncomfortable with his success in Gaul. He decided to tackle things head on, first inviting Crassus and then Pompey to a meeting at Lucca in Etruria, at that time part of Cisalpine Gaul. Here they discussed their various issues, reaching a consensus that allowed the triumvirate to be renewed. Specifically, Crassus and Pompey were to stand for consul in 55 BC and once elected confirm the extension of Caesar's command in Gaul by another five years. Then, at the close of their consular year, Crassus would become proconsul in Syria where he expected to boost his already fabulous wealth, while Pompey would keep control of Roman Spain.

Gaul and Germany again

His political fortunes set on a solid footing again, Caesar headed north once more. This time his targets were the tribes along the Atlantic freeboard. These had seized Roman officers there collecting provisions for Caesar's eight legions further south, this sparking a full rebellion.

The threat to the Romans here was on a smaller scale than in 58 BC or 57 BC and for once Caesar split his army, sending some legions north and some south. He himself took the largest force to attack the Veneti, a large tribe on the coast of Armorica. These were noted seafarers who controlled maritime trade with Britain, and for this campaign Caesar raised a fleet of war galleys in the Mediterranean. These were deployed to the northwest European coast where they overcame the Veneti fleet of some 220 vessels at the battle of Morbihan Gulf in late summer. The Romans displayed their usual military ingenuity here, using sickle-shaped hooks on the end of long poles to cut the rigging of the Veneti vessels which were much more suitable for conflict in the regional sea conditions. This was because they had a much higher freeboard than the Roman galleys, a lesson learned by the Romans for their later campaigns in Britain. The remaining Veneti ships were then scattered and picked off one by one along the coast of Brittany, the Roman galleys being more manoeuvrable there. With the destruction of their fleet Veneti sued for peace, though Caesar imposed a very harsh penalty for their rebellion, beheading their entire ruling council.

The result of the Roman campaigns elsewhere along the coast was equally successful, with only the Menapii and Morani refusing to submit to Rome, and soon the region was broadly at peace again.

Caesar again wintered in Cisalpine Gaul. The following spring in 55 BC word reached him that a new German migration was underway. This was the Usipetes and Tencteri tribes from the eastern bank of the River Rhine. Some 430,000 had crossed into Gaul, fleeing predations by the Suebi. Caesar headed north immediately to join his eight legions. Once there he met a delegation from the Germans who requested asylum in Gaul. Caesar refused, suggesting that the two tribes share the land of the Ubii, another German tribe on the eastern bank of the Rhine hostile to the Suebi. The Usipetes and Tencteri delegations asked for three days to consider this. While under truce, an engagement of some kind then broke out between the Roman Gallic allied cavalry and the German cavalry defending their nearby camp. Caesar took this to be treachery, and he decided the Germans were spinning out the negotiations to gain a military advantage. The following day he therefore ordered an all-out attack on the German camp, catching the entire Usipetes and Tencteri tribes by surprise. What followed was a massacre rather than a military engagement, with recent archaeological finds near the battle site at Kessel in the Netherlands indicating as many as 200,000 may have perished. No Roman casualties are recorded. Such was the scale of the slaughter here that his opponents in the Senate back in Rome seized on it to attack him as a barbarian. However, Caesar seems to have revelled in the brutality. For him the actions had prevented another occurrence similar to the Suebi incursions in 57 BC that had cost so many Roman and allied Gallic lives. He ignored the criticism and decided on a show of strength to deter any further German incursions into Gaul. For the first time he would cross the Rhine into Germany proper.

To do this Caesar relied on the engineering skills of his legionaries. He ordered the building of a substantial wooden bridge downstream of modern Koblenz between Andernach and Neuwied. This used double timber pilings, each of 45cm thickness, which were rammed into the riverbed every 60cm using a large winched stone as a hammer. They were deliberately slanted inwards, and then secured using a crossbeam. Numerous such units were linked up to form the supports for the bridge. A wooden roadway was then laid across them. Further pilings were then set upstream. These acted as a protective barrier for the bridge against damage from anything flowing downstream, deliberately or otherwise. Finally guard towers were built at either end to secure the crossing point. The bridge was up to 400m in length and 9m wide, built 'in a few days'. However, this great feat of engineering skills came to nought. The local German tribes, including the Suebi who were the real target of the offensive, had evacuated their lands. Caesar therefore ravaged them for 18 days to cement the message given the earlier incursion of the Usipetes and Tencteri into Gaul, before returning back across the Rhine. His last action here was the burn the bridge his troops had just built.

Britain

There was still time in the campaigning season of 55 BC for Caesar to seek out new opponents. With Gaul largely pacified he therefore turned his attention to his most outlandish target yet, mysterious and mythical Britain. It is hard to explain today to a modern audience what a fantastical adventure he planned here. In the first instance his force would have to cross Oceanus, a sea frightful to contemporary audiences who were used to the comparatively benign Mediterranean. Then once there he would be campaigning in a land of which the Romans knew little, other than the few pieces of intelligence provided by Mediterranean merchants and geographers from the previous few centuries. This was truly a leap in the dark, and it is worth considering for a moment why Caesar thought it worth the effort.

In the first instance Britain remained a source of instability in Gaul. The Cantiaci in Kent were only 33 km from the nearest point of Gallia Belgica across the English Channel, while a number of other British tribes had direct links with counterparts in Gaul. Some even shared a name, for example the Belgae on the south coast, Atrebates in the Thames Valley and Parisii above the Humber. One can be sure that the tribes in Britain became host to increasingly large numbers of refugees, particularly tribal elites, as Caesar ground his way across Gaul from 58 BC. These and their descendants would continue to be a thorn in the side of Roman Gaul until the Claudian invasion of Britain began in AD 43.

Caesar would also have known that Britain was rich in raw materials, this being one of the few facts recorded about the islands at the time. He himself notes that 'Tin is found inland, and small quantities of iron near the coast' (*The Conquest of Gaul*, V.2). Meanwhile, the Greek geographer Strabo later wrote of iron being an export from Britain (The Geography, IV.5). Britain was also known for its export of woollen goods, hunting dogs and – interestingly – slaves. The latter indicates that tribal relations in Britain were far from stable, adding to the Roman sense of instability there.

Finally, and perhaps most importantly, Britain presented Caesar with his ultimate challenge. He was a man driven by destiny and a need for prestige amongst both peers and the popular classes back in Rome, as well as with his legionaries. This begs the question of whether he actually intended to conquer the islands, or simply make a dramatic and bold statement. I believe that latter and think his two incursions of late 55 BC and 54 BC were in fact large-scale armed reconnaissances. They will therefore be considered as such here.

For the first attempt in 55 BC Caesar marched his legionaries from *legio* VII and *legio* X north to the territory of the Morini

Pegwell Bay, Kent. During Caesar's two incursions to Britain in 55 and 54 BC this bay would have been filled with war galleys and merchants' ships. (John Lambshead)

opposite Kent. Here he gathered a fleet of 80 transports and 18 other vessels, the latter modified to carry horses. To these he added the war galleys recently used against the Veneti. He then sent the experienced tribune Caius Volusenus in a trireme to identify a safe landing area on the east Kent coast. Caesar then waited for favourable weather conditions before crossing. His fleet arrived in late August off Dover, although his cavalry transports missed the tide and were never to arrive in Britain.

When the Romans arrived they found native British troops massed on the coast awaiting their arrival, bolstered by Gallic refugees. Caesar wanted to avoid a contested landing and headed north, with his fleet eventually weighing anchor between Walmer and Pegwell Bay below Ramsgate. However, the Britons had followed his fleet up the coast and once again deployed along the shore to challenge him. He was therefore forced to carry out a full amphibious assault. For this he drove his war galleys hard ashore to the north of the landing beaches, aiming to turn the Britons' right flank. From this position the war galleys enfiladed the landing area with ballista, bows and slings to try to drive the Britons from the shore. However, even with this covering fire his legionaries were reluctant to land. An iconic incident now occurred when the *aquilifer* of *legio* X, carrying the legion's *aquila* eagle standard, leapt into the shallows declaring, 'Leap, fellow soldiers, unless you wish to betray your eagle to the enemy. I, for my part, will perform my duty to the Republic and to my general' (*The Conquest of Gaul*, V.1).

The shamed legionaries now swarmed ashore to protect their eagle, this taking longer than expected given that the larger transports struggled to get close to the beach as their design was unsuitable in these northern waters. Once on the beach and engaged in hand-to-hand combat the legionaries were quickly successful and the Britons sued for peace, bringing the battle to a swift end. However bad weather later damaged many of Caesar's ships and, after some unspecified regional campaigning, the Romans returned to the Continent using the remaining serviceable vessels.

Our best insight into this first campaign comes from marching camp crop marks left in the archaeological record. Some of the best examples from across the Empire are to be found in Britain, especially in Wales and Scotland. However, until recently Caesar's campaigns in Britain proved problematic given there were no recorded marching camps in Kent. Thankfully this has recently been addressed through the finding of a 20 ha marching camp at Pegwell Bay. Here, archaeologists have uncovered a defensive ditched enclosure that was very similar to those used in Caesar's later siege of Alesia in Gaul. Further, a *pilum* head was found in it in context with mid-1st century BC pottery. This has been interpreted as evidence of Caesar's first incursion.

Although Caesar doesn't reference the first incursion as a failure, the fact that he decided to return in 54 BC indicates that he viewed his British enterprise as unfinished business. Thus early in that year he gathered five legions, a much bigger force, and 2,000 cavalry. It is worth noting here that, as referenced earlier, in both his British campaigns he didn't use his entire

Aylesford on the Medway from Bluebell Hill, the crossing point of the river during the later Claudian invasion and possible crossing place for Caesar's second incursion in 54 BC.

army as he normally did when campaigning in Gaul. This is another indicator that his interests here weren't occupation but to scout the islands in force, perhaps with a view to a later return. He had also learned from his 55 BC incursion regarding the type of vessel best suited for amphibious operations in Britain as he ordered the construction of 600 specially built ships featuring lower freeboards than his Mediterranean designs to enable easier disembarkation, and wider beams to carry bulkier loads. To these he added 200 locally chartered transports, over 80 ships that had survived the previous year's incursion and his 28 remaining war galleys.

This bigger force intimidated the Briton's and the Roman landing on the east coast of Kent was this time unopposed. Just as in 55 BC however, bad weather intervened. While Caesar was campaigning inland against a large British force that had eventually gathered to confront the Romans, a heavy storm badly damaged many of Caesar's transports anchored off the Kentish coast. Realising the danger of being stranded, he left a holding force facing the Britons and quickly returned to the landing area. Here he initiated urgent repairs, with many of the vessels being dragged onto the beach to prevent further damage in the bad weather. The legions then renewed their campaign against the Britons, with legionary spearheads forcing a crossing of the Thames supported by war galleys. He then captured the main base of the British leader Cassivellaunus who promptly sued for peace. Roman honour satisfied, Caesar returned to the landing zone in Kent and re-embarked his forces. These returned to northeastern Gaul in two waves because of the scale of ship losses in the earlier storm. The first travelled to the continent safely, but these vessels were prevented from returning by more bad weather. Caesar then decided to risk packing his remaining troops onto the few serviceable vessels left in Briton, the war galleys that had supported his Thames operation. These arrived back safely at the end of September, and thus ended Caesar's engagements in Britain.

Caesar again gathered his scribes to report what he described as his successes in Britain back to Rome in a new series of commentaries. However, the year ended on two very sad family notes, the first of which had major political repercussions. This was because in August his daughter Julia, the wife of Pompey, died while in childbirth. Their baby died shortly afterwards. He was close to Julia and felt her death keenly. It also cut one of the key ties that linked the two triumvirs together. Meanwhile, in the same year his mother Aurelia also passed away, an event he would have felt equally acutely.

Rebellion

While Caesar wintered again in Cisalpine Gaul discontent grew among the subjugated Gauls to the north. This erupted in a major rebellion by the Eburones tribe in Gallia Belgica, led by their leader Ambiorix. Here fifteen Roman cohorts were quartered in a major camp, led by the legates Lucius Aurunculeius Cotta and Quintus Titurius Sabinus. They included the entire *legio* XIV.

As soon as the revolt began the camp was attacked but the Gauls were repulsed. Ambiorix now offered the Romans safe passage south to join other nearby Roman forces. Cotta and Sabinus argued over this, the former saying their orders from Caesar were to remain where they were in their well-protected and provisioned camp. However, the latter argued they should accept the offer and he prevailed. Early the following morning the camp was struck and the cohorts of legionaries left in good order. Sadly for the Romans it was yet another Gallic trap, the column being ambushed near modern Tongeren in Belgium. It was wiped out almost to a man, despite fighting valiantly. Satisfied with their good work, the Eburones returned to their towns and villages with any loot they could gather from the destroyed Roman cohorts.

The rebellion was far from over however. Not to be outdone, the Nervii now rebelled against the Roman troops based in their land to the north of the Eburones. Here they besieged a Roman legion in its camp under the command of the legate Quintus Tullius Cicero, younger brother of the great statesman back in Rome. Caesar sped north to their rescue with as many of his troops as he could muster, arriving just in time to save them and prevent the loss of another legion. He then mounted punitive campaigns against the Eburones, Nervii and the other Gallia Belgica tribes, characteristically wiping out all of the rebels. He also mounted another expedition against the Suebi to prevent their interference, building a further wooden bridge across the Rhine, though the Germans again retreated and no action took place. Soon the region was pacified once more.

Back in Rome more political developments were now taking place which marked the effective end of the triumvirate. The first one was very final indeed, with Crassus being killed while leading his legions east against the Parthians. The second was Pompey declining an offer of marriage to Caesar's great-niece. From now on, the leaders of the *optimates* and *populares* factions were increasingly be at odds, matters coming to a head as the decade ended. This set the seen for the subsequent bitter civil wars of the AD 40s.

Vercingetorix was the son Celtillus, king of the Gallic Averni tribe. He became the leader after his father was executed by Avernian nobles for attempting to become king of all of the Gauls. Vercingetorix then led the general uprising of Gauls against Caesar in 52 BC, becoming the general of the confederated Gallic peoples who grouped together to overthrow Roman rule. After initial setbacks he resorted to guerrilla warfare, but later defeated Caesar at the Battle of Gergovia, an Avernian hill-fort. Here the Romans lost several thousand troops. A follow up attack failed however and he withdrew to Alesia, this battle and its outcome detailed below.

Caesar wintered in Cisalpine Gaul again over 53 BC and 52 BC, where he raised a new *legio* XIV to replace that lost and also created the new *legio* XV. Given the size of his army now, and the scale of his butchery of the rebels in the previous campaigning season, he believed Gaul would now settle quietly into Roman provincial life. That was far from the case, with much worse to come. The Gallic tribes remained rebellious and now found a new leader in Vercingetorix, king of the Arverni tribe in Gallia Centrica, around whom resistance now coalesced.

In 52 BC a mass revolt erupted across Gaul, prompting Caesar to quickly target the Arverni capital Gergovia in the hope of halting the rebellion early. This first attack was repulsed, but Caesar now ordered a prolonged campaign which eventually forced Vercingetorix and 60,000 of his warriors to seek shelter in the fortified hilltop town of Alesia, capital of the Mandubii tribe in Gallia Centrica.

Caesar decided to starve Vercingetorix into surrender, with what followed a classic example of Roman prowess in siege warfare. First he ordered his men to construct ditches and an earthen

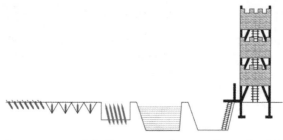

A cross-section of the Roman siege lines at Alesia. (Paul Baker)

bank topped with a palisade, similar to the technique used to build marching camps but far grander in scale. When finished this was an astonishing 18 km long, interspersed with timber towers which enabled the legionaries and archers to enfilade anyone attacking the front or rear. The huge circuit enclosed the town in a circumvallation. Caesar's detailed accounts (*The Conquest of Gaul*, VII, 5) of his campaign against Vercingetorix provide very detailed descriptions of the siege works. The bank and palisade was 3.6m in height, featuring sharpened forked branches which projected outwards towards Alesia. Beyond this two ditches were dug, both 4.4m wide and 2.4m deep. The one nearer the bank and palisade had ankle breakers in the bottom, these being steps cut into the base which were designed to trap the feet of any attackers scrambling to get up the other side, snapping the ankle bones. The ditch set further out was lined with clay, allowing it to be filled with water. Even further out, another shallow trench 1.5m deep was dug in which was set five rows of sharpened stakes. Beyond these, a formation of pits up to 1m wide in repeating *quincunx* formation (four in the corners of a square and one in the centre) was set out, each with another stake. These were concealed, being nicknamed lilies. Finally, even further out, a band of *stimuli* wooden blocks with iron barbs were set in the ground, the Roman equivalent of a modern minefield.

A stimuli. (Paul Baker)

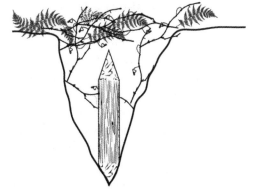

A 'lilly'. (Paul Baker)

Vercingetorix responded with constant raids against the Roman legionaries constructing the circumvallation but failed to slow progress. However, as construction neared completion a large force of Gallic cavalry burst through the defences and made off into the surrounding countryside. Caesar correctly guessed they had been sent to fetch assistance and now began constructing a second ditch, bank and palisade fortification to the rear of the first. This matched the one facing Alesia and, at 22km long, was even longer. It faced outward to cover his rear and formed a contravallation. There was only one area of weakness in this new wall, a section where a deep ravine and large boulders made it impossible to build a continuous fortification. Caesar therefore masked the spot using a kink in the wall.

Gallic warriors on the charge.

Next, an incident occurred which again showed Caesar at his most brutal and resolute. Vercingetorix tried to save whatever food and water remained for his warriors by forcing all of the women and children in Alesia out through its gates and towards the Roman lines. He hoped they would let them pass through, but badly miscalculated. Caesar refused, and they had no choice but to camp between the town and the fortifications where they slowly starved.

Then in late September a Gallic relief army finally arrived. It immediately launched an attack on the contravallation outer wall. Vercingetorix coordinated with an attack from Alesia itself against the circumvallation inner wall. The legions fought off both attacks but the assaults were renewed the following night, and continued over the next few days. The Roman besiegers now found themselves the besieged between their two siege lines. Matters came to a head on the 2nd of October when the Gauls attacked the weak spot in the Roman outer wall. Vercingetorix again coordinated with an assault against the inner wall. Caesar realised the dual attacks would be difficult to defend against and poured in reinforcements, also distracting Vercingetorix by sallying legionaries out into the open in front of Alesia. Despite heroic efforts in both areas Caesar now saw both lines were in danger of cracking. Therefore, to save the day he again showed great personal bravery by leading his 6,000 allied cavalry from the outer walls. These charged the rear of the Gallic foot there as they assaulted the palisade. Trapped

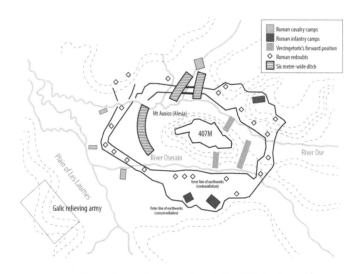

Caesar's siege lines at Alesia. (Paul Baker)

against the fortification, they were butchered. The survivors broke and ran, the pursuing Roman cavalry causing even more slaughter. Eventually the Gallic camp was overrun.

Vercingetorix knew he was defeated and tried to negotiate with Caesar who, keen to end the revolt, agreed to spare the lives of his men. The Gallic leader then surrendered and the siege ended. Vercingetorix was less fortunate than his men though, being sent to Rome in chains. This was a dramatic fall from grace, the deposed king held captive for five years before finally forming the centrepiece of Caesar's triumph in Rome when he was executed by strangulation.

Caesar's work in Gaul was now done. He'd raised his final two legions there – the native Gallic *legio* V *Alaudae* and also *legio* VI – to finish things off in 52 BC and help any mopping up operations in 51 BC. Now he turned his attention back to Rome where his political agents were already in place and working on his behalf, buying political support with the wealth accrued from his conquest of Gaul.

CHAPTER 5

CIVIL WAR

Even with the conquest of Gaul Caesar still hadn't reached the final heady heights for which history best remembers him. These included his dramatic campaign against Pompey and his supporters during the civil wars that followed the Gallic campaigns, his famous dalliance with the Ptolemaic queen Cleopatra, and finally his assassination on the steps of the (temporary) Senate House on the Ides in March 44 BC at the hands of those who thought him the arch enemy of the Republic. These are all considered in turn here.

Crossing the Rubicon

Caesar's main issue now was the demise of the triumvirate. While it existed the three most powerful men in Rome were kept in balance and check. Not everyone approved, and both Crassus and Pompey had become increasingly suspicious of Caesar's military success – at least as he reported it – in Gaul. But crucially, civil war between the *optimates* and *populares* had been averted. Now, with Crassus dead and Pompey estranged, the balance of power between the two factions quickly spun out of control.

The specific problem facing Caesar was exactly the same as it had been when he left for Gaul in 58 BC. This was his vulnerability to private prosecution by his political enemies once out of office. While a proconsul in Gaul and Illyricum he was immune from this, and once he again became a consul back in Rome he would also be immune. The time gap between was where he was susceptible to attack. If subject to legal action then, he might be financially ruined. He knew there were plenty of *optimates* in Rome willing to try and make their names taking on the conqueror of Gaul. He therefore needed to keep one of his provinces until he became a consul again.

This issue had already been the subject of much political maneuvering in Rome. Caesar had had his pro-consulships extended by a further five years at the Conference of Luca in 56 BC. Now that extension was coming to an end, just at the time when his Gallic conquests were also ending, making a further five-year extension unlikely. He did think he had part solved the problem during Pompey's consulship in 52 BC when a law was passed which allowed him to stand for the consulship *in absentia* while in Gaul. This was set for the elections in 49 BC, with the aim of him being consul in 48 BC. The timing of his leaving Gaul and Illyricum and then becoming consul still left him 10 months short however, when he would be vulnerable to his enemies. Despite the increasing tensions with Pompey, an agreement seems to have been reached to mitigate this in the form of an understanding that no debates in the Senate to find a successor in Caesar's provinces would begin until the 1st of March 50 BC. However, with the cracks in his relationship with Pompey widening by the day, these debates actually began as early as 51 BC. Each time they had to be voted down by Caesar's supporters, led by Mark Antony who now comes to the fore in Caesar's story for the first time.

Mark Antony was born in 83 BC into the plebeian Antonia clan. After a slow start on the *cursus honorum* he served with distinction between 57 BC and 55 BC as a cavalry commander in Judea and Egypt. He was then transferred to Gaul where he joined

Caesar's personal staff, the two being related on Mark Antony's mother's side. In 52 BC he returned to Rome as a quaestor with responsibility for financial administration, the post giving him a lifetime seat in the Senate. It was from this position that he now became the chief defender of Caesar in Rome.

Despite his best efforts, the issue finally came to a head in 50 BC when Gaius Claudius Marcellus, one of the consuls that year, had a resolution passed in the Senate saying that Caesar should lay down command of his provinces on the official final date, with no extensions. Mark Antony and Caesar's many *populares* supporters moved to block this again, and on the 1st of December Caesar's backer Gaius Scribonius Curio managed to obtain a resolution of 370 votes to 22 specifying both Caesar and Pompey lay down their pro-consulships at the same time. The game was now afoot. The following day, without any authorisation from the Senate, Marcellus made Pompey an offer to take command of all of the legions in Italy, with the ability to raise more legionaries if he wished. Pompey immediately accepted and Caesar, still in Cisalpine Gaul, now realised conflict was inevitable. He decided to act first to catch the *optimates* off guard and provoke the coming fight, writing to the Senate on the 1st of January 49 BC to say he would only resign his commands at a time of his choosing. He knew this tone would infuriate his opponents, and the Senate quickly declared he would be treated as a public enemy if he didn't lay down his commands on a date to be fixed by them. He was also specifically told not to bring his troops across the Rubicon river just north of Ravenna which separated Cisalpine Gaul from Italy proper. This was all Caesar needed to make his move. On the 11th of January he led *legio* XIII *Gemina* across the shallow waterway, declaring *alea iacta est* (the die is cast) after a famous quote by the Athenian playwright Menander. When the legion was over he led them south for Rome at high speed. This was a clear act of war, and once more the *optimates* and *populares* would come to blows.

When he received word of Caesar's lightning strike Pompey fled Rome and headed south as fast as possible to the port of

Brindisi (Roman *Brundisium*) on the Adriatic Sea. While his army heavily outnumbered Caesar's single legion, he believed some of his own troops would side with the *populares* when their champion arrived. He knew that his most loyal veterans were in Greece, so he headed there. Caesar pursued and almost caught Pompey and his troops, but they just escaped. He now returned to Rome, facing down any *optimates* opposition. Caesar was ever a pragmatic strategist and knew he would have to secure his rear before he chased Pompey across the Adriatic. The latter also had a strong power base in Spain where he remained proconsul, including seven legions. Caesar now targeted these in a rapid offensive that lasted until August 49 BC.

To ensure surprise he marched his legions day and night through Provincia, taking only 27 days to reach the Pyrenees. Speed was of the essence and he allowed nothing to stand in his way. When he reached the key city of Marseille (Roman *Massilia*) it rebelled under the leading Pompeian Lucius Domitius Ahenobarbus. Caesar marched straight past, leaving behind two of his *legates* with allied troops to besiege the port. He then sent three legions ahead of his main column under the *legate* Fabius to seize the Pyrenean mountain passes from Pompey's troops. This ensured a swift entry into Hispania Citerior where he reformed the army and headed south.

Most of the Pompeian legions chose to make a stand on a hill near Lleida (Roman Ilerda) in northeastern Catalonia, led by the *legates* Petreius and Afranius. When Caesar arrived he initially declined battle, halting short of the hill and deploying his first two lines in case of a surprise attack. He then deployed his third line out of sight of the Pompeians, and they dug a deep ditch behind which he withdrew the first two lines after nightfall. He then kept his troops under arms overnight to guard against a surprise attack, the following day turning the ditch into a substantial fortified camp.

Caesar now scouted the wider area and found a hill that was occupied by Petreius and Afrianus and the town. He realised that if he occupied it he would block the Pompeian army from their lines of supply to the town. He sent swift detachments towards the new hill, with the Pompeian's countering with their own column. The latter, comprised of skirmishers, arrived first and used their missile weapons to drive off Caesar's initial force. However the Pompeians then pursued too far and were caught be Caesar's *legio* IX which routed them and drove them to the walls of Lleida. Now Caesar's legionaries pursued too far and were in turn counter-attacked as they occupied yet another hill, this time beneath the town walls. Here a general meeting engagement developed with the Caesarians at a disadvantage due to terrain that allowed the Pompeians to feed in a greater troop numbers. *Legio* IX, and the various detachments sent in to support them, fought bravely however, holding their ground for five hours. The Pompeian legionaries eventually tired. Sensing this, Caesar ordered his troops to charge with drawn swords, breaking the *optimates* army. The survivors fled back to the town and their own camp.

A protracted stand off followed through the spring, with the Pompeians staying behind the town walls and in camp, and Caesar's troops remaining in their own camp. The latter, on lower terrain, particularly suffered from mountain stream seasonal flooding. Once the weather improved however, Caesar again formed up and offered battle. This time the Pompeians chose to withdraw, aiming to join up with another Republican force under Marcus Terentius Varro. Caesar again responded swiftly, overtaking their rearguard and forcing the retreating army to build another marching camp. Caesar then moved to their rear aiming to block their line of retreat. This forced the Pompeians to return to Lleida. Caesar now surrounded the town and began a full siege, his intelligence sources reporting morale among the opposing legionaries was poor. Finally, on the 2nd of August, the five Pompeian legions there surrendered. Caesar kept up the campaign momentum, now marching south into Hispania Ulterior where he'd raised his elite *legio* X while proconsul. His old province immediately submitted and Pompey's final two legions in Spain surrendered. The campaign was over. Leaving four legions in Spain to deter any future revolt, he now turned his attention to Pompey in Greece.

Greece and Pharsalus

There the *optimates* champion had made Veria (ancient Greek Beroea) in Thessaly his headquarters, mustering nine legions and many allied troops. The latter included cavalry, archers and slingers. He also gathered a large fleet of 600 ships. Back in Italy Caesar appointed Mark Antony to control the Senate and began to gather an invasion force.

Pompey got word of his plans and moved his legions to the western coast of Greece to counter any landing. When nothing happened by the end of the campaigning season he moved his troops into winter quarters. However, on the 4th of January 48 BC Caesar surprised all by mustering all the troops he had to make a surprise winter crossing of the Adriatic, even leaving his baggage train behind to save time. They avoided Pompey's Corfu-based fleet and landed without incident at Palasë (ancient Greek Palaestra) in Illyria. To draw Pompey's army out of their winter camps Caesar then began sacking the nearby cities that were nominally under Pompey's protection. The tactic worked and the Republican army moved to intercept Caesar, the two armies then facing off either side of the River Apsus. There they remained for four months, waiting for the campaigning season to begin.

In April Mark Antony arrived with reinforcements, boosting the number of Caesar's legions to 11. These included his own and those which had come over to the *populares* side in Italy. The two forces now broke camp, Pompey heading back to Thessaly and Caesar following. There they faced off again at Asparagium. Despite still outnumbering Caesar, many of whose legions were understrength, Pompey still refused to engage in battle, confident he could interdict Caesar's lines of supply. Pompey then moved on once more, this time back to the west coast at Dyrrachium. Caesar now began an audacious project to build an enclosing wall around Pompey's camp, aiming to box it in against the sea. Quickly realising the danger Pompey countered, sallying out with his troops, forcing Caesar to retreat. The Republican leader then established a new camp south of Caesar's siege lines, threatening his rear. However, on the 9th of July when Pompey's forces were split between Dyrrachium and the new camp, Caesar attacked the former. Pompey was forced to send five of his legions to rescue the trapped troops. Both sides suffered heavy losses, particularly Caesar, though the action proved indecisive.

Caesar now abandoned his blockade and withdrew to the south, concerned at the increasing disparity in numbers as Pompey continued to receive reinforcements from his allies in Anatolia and the east. Pompey's cavalry pursued the withdrawal but Caesar escaped towards the east coast. On the way he set up camp on the north bank of the River Enipeus between Pharsalus and Palaepharsalus in central Greece. Pompey followed, setting up his own camp 1km to the west. For this the latter chose a range of low hills that provided a good strategic position and ensured a safe route for supplies to reach him from the coast. The two armies again faced off again.

Both armies here featured the usual core of legions supported by allies, though Pompey had the larger army and more allies. By this stage in the campaign Caesar had elements of nine legions with him, numbering around 23,000 legionaries in 80 cohorts. He also had up to 10,000 allied foot and 1,000 Gallic and German cavalry. Pompey had elements of 12 legions, like Caesar's some understrength, together with seven cohorts of legionaries from Spain who'd escaped Caesar there. All told these numbered some 50,000 legionaries, to which he added 4,200 allied foot and 7,000 allied horse.

Caesar was keen to settle the issue immediately. Pompey however, encamped on the range of hills, was unwilling to abandon his advantage of high ground even though the weight of numbers was in his favour. Several days passed before Caesar decided to try to draw Pompey from his camp by falling back. On the 9th of August Pompey took the bait and moved his troops out onto the plain. Caesar moved forward immediately, abandoning his baggage and even destroying the field defences of his camp to get more of his legionaries onto the battlefield.

Pompey was first to deploy, with his 110 cohorts plus allies lined up along a 4km front in the standard triple line formation. He then positioned most of his cavalry, archers and slingers on his left flank up hard against the low hills next to his camp, with a smaller cavalry and light infantry force on the right set against the River Enipeus. His veteran legionaries were dispersed throughout his force to support the many newly recruited troops. Pompey's battle plan was for his cavalry to circle behind Caesar's flanks and then attack his rear while the infantry pinned his centre. He positioned himself at the rear of the left wing.

Caesar cannily deployed somewhat later, lining up his troops parallel to Pompey's but with his three lines thinner given his numerical disadvantage. Next he positioned himself opposite Pompey, behind the elite *legio* X. He then deployed his cavalry on the right, and to harass Pompey's legionaries, his light missile troops across his centre. As a precaution against Pompey's superior cavalry numbers he also positioned six cohorts of legionaries as a reserve on his extreme right flank at an oblique angle.

The battle of Pharsalus now began. Both armies closed to within 140m and faced off. Pompey ordered the first attack, using his cavalry where he held the numerical advantage. Caesar's cavalry counter-charged and a sharp melee ensued. Meanwhile, Caesar's first two lines of infantry approached Pompey's centre. However, the legionaries there stood their ground rather than advance to meet them. Seeing Pompey's lines were not moving, Caesar halted his legions just out of range of their lighter *pila*. He then redressed ranks, before ordering a charge by his first two lines, the third being held in reserve. The legionaries surged forward, each unleashing both *pila* before drawing their *gladius* and closing. Pompey's legionaries counter-charged, both sides finally meeting in a savage impact.

On the left flank Pompey's cavalry were making their weight of numbers tell and Caesar ordered his mounted troops to withdraw. This left Pompey in control of that flank. However Caesar now ordered his right flank reserve of six cohorts of legionaries to move forward to engage Pompey's cavalry, who were reforming after the melee there. They charged to close quarters, hurling their *pila* into the faces of the cavalrymen who broke in short order. The Republican cavalry fled the field in confusion. This left Caesar in control of the whole flank.

In the centre Caesar now committed his third line to prevent Pompey from deploying his own legionaries to cover the latter's exposed flank. He then neatly wheeled the six cohorts on his right into the exposed left flank of Pompey's legions. Butchery followed and Pompey's army broke, the allied troops fleeing first before the legionaries. The latter, under constant attack, now retreated headlong, with Pompey himself falling back to his camp. He remained there for a short while but, seeing the battle was now beyond recovery, then fled the field completely. He rode for Larissa with a small escort, disguising himself as an ordinary soldier to avoid detection by Caesar's cavalry patrols.

Caesar was relentless in his pursuit of Pompey's army, wiping out his camp and then chasing what was left of his legions to a nearby hill called the Kaloyiros. This he besieged, and eventually Pompey's leaderless troops surrendered. Caesar claimed to have killed 15,000 of Pompey's soldiers, while losing only 1,200 himself. Pompey never recovered, fleeing to Egypt to seek sanctuary with the Ptolemaic boy co-regent Ptolemy XIII who had been his supporter. No doubt to his great surprise, when he landed in the Egyptian capital of Alexandria he was summarily beheaded.

Egypt

Caesar knew he would have to capture or kill Pompey before the civil war could end and promptly set sail for Egypt with a small squadron. Here the Ptolemaic dynasty continued its rule, with the young Ptolemy and Cleopatra VII joint rulers following the death of their father Ptolemy XII Auletes. Both had their own armies and strove to be sole ruler, with the former now in poll position given his links with Pompey. However, it was also Ptolemy who'd ordered Pompey's execution as he'd arrived fleeing Caesar. This had been at the suggestion of his guardian and key advisor, the eunuch Pothinus. The latter had received news of the outcome of Pharsalus before Pompey's arrival and thought the beheading would endear Ptolemy to Caesar.

The boy now sailed out to meet Caesar, presenting him with the severed head of his great rival aboard the Roman flagship. If he and Pothinus were expecting gratitude however they were rudely awakened. Caesar was incandescent, demanding to know why a minor Hellenistic despot thought it fit to murder one of the leading men of Rome. Caesar repaid the affront by announcing he would enact the will of Ptolemy XII. This would be to the detriment of Ptolemy XIII and Pothinus as it reinforced the co-regency with Cleopatra. Pothinus realised this and stirred up the mob in Alexandria against the Romans to deter Caesar from landing ashore. He typically ignored them and arrived on the harbor front with a small force of legionaries that formed into a column and headed directly to the Palace. There he confronted both co-regents, insisting they disband their armies and reminding them they owed him money. This was the better part of 10 million *denarii* promised to Caesar by Ptolemy XII a decade earlier when Caesar was beginning his wars in Gaul. Pothinus kept his counsel here but afterwards quietly engaged with Achilles, commander of the main Ptolemaic army, to prepare for action against the Romans. Meanwhile, because of the fate of Pompey, Caesar now began to favour Cleopatra who moved ahead of her younger brother in the regency pecking order. Shortly afterwards the two became lovers.

Cleopatra VII was one of the most enigmatic figures in world history. She was the final ruler of the Ptolemaic dynasty, reigning from 51 BC to 30 BC. Celebrated in contemporary sources for her beauty and intellect, she is most famous for her love affairs with Julius Caesar and Mark Antony. She was born in 69 BC, the daughter of Ptolemy XII who died in 51 BC. Cleopatra then became the co-regent with her 10-year-old brother Ptolemy XIII whom she married. This was in keeping with Ptolemaic Egyptian royal tradition. Her role in the Alexandrian War, relationship with Caesar and birth of their son Caesarion are detailed below. After Caesar's death, she later began her romantic liaison with Mark Antony who at the time was in dispute with Octavian over the Roman leadership succession. They had three children, two sons and a daughter. In 31 BC their combined armies were defeated at the Battle of Actium on the west coast of Greece by Octavian. Cleopatra and Mark Antony then fled back to Egypt, pursued by Octavian who in 30 BC captured Alexandria. With his soldiers deserting him, Mark Antony then took his own life, famously followed by Cleopatra on the 12th of August that year.

Matters now quickly came to a head. When Ptolemy arrived for a meeting with Caesar he found Cleopatra with him. He promptly stormed out and ordered Pothinus to again raise the Alexandrian mob, this time against not only the Romans but also his sister. Caesar used his famous skills in rhetoric to calm the crowd, reading out the will of the dead king, announcing yet again that Ptolemy XIII and Cleopatra would be co- regents, and adding that Rhodes would be returned to Egyptian rule by the Romans. He knew the latter would make him even more unpopular with the *optimates* back in Rome, but correctly judged it would help win over the Alexandrians.

A banquet was now arranged to celebrate the newly founded, Roman sponsored peace between brother and sister. However, during the dinner Caesar received word that Pothinus and Achillas were plotting against him and Cleopatra. The eunuch was executed there and then, though the latter escaped and rallied Ptolemy's army and the Alexandrian city guard who surrounded the palace. So began the Alexandrian War.

Caesar, with only the force of legionaries he had landed with, decided to fortify the palace and a siege began. Inside he held not only Cleopatra but also Ptolemy XIII and their younger sister Arsinoe. He had more troops still aboard ship just outside the harbour with his fast squadron, but these wouldn't be enough to mount a rescue if Achilles ordered the palace to be stormed. However, he also knew that a much larger force with much of his army was following his own rapid crossing, and would be there soon. He also knew that Achilles, an experienced commander, would attempt to stop this new force arriving. Caesar acted first, ordering the burning of the Ptolemaic fleet in the harbour. This set fire to some nearby warehouses and in the confusion Arsinoe fled, joining Achilles who now declared her to be the new queen. They quickly fell out however and Achilles was beheaded, to be replaced by Ganymedes, another court eunuch and her former tutor.

Ganymedes now ordered that the water supply to the palace be poisoned in the hope of forcing Caesar and Cleopatra's surrender. The queen countered by having new wells cut. Caesar then released Ptolemy, hoping it would destabilise the relationship between Arsinoe and Ganymede. It had the opposite effect, revitalising the anti-Cleopatra faction just at the point when their campaign was beginning to slow. At this point, when all seemed lost for Caesar and Cleopatra, she revealed to him that she was pregnant by him.

Then, at the last minute, all was saved when Caesar's main reinforcements arrived. They landed on the causeway linking the famous lighthouse in Alexandria to the harbour and a fierce battle took place there. Another Roman force then landed south of Alexandria and Ptolemy now turned his forces about and headed off to meet them. Caesar, having joined his legionaries on the harbour front in Alexandria, pursued them vigorously and the Ptolemaic army was caught in a pincer movement. In short order it was defeated with heavy losses, with Ptolemy himself drowning in the Nile. Caesar returned to Alexandria with the body to be met by Cleopatra, where another younger brother was proclaimed her new co-regent as Ptolemy XIV. To celebrate their victory Caesar and Cleopatra then carried out a triumphal voyage up the Nile with 400 vessels.

When they returned to Alexandria, no doubt Caesar took time to view the body of his hero Alexander the Great in its *souma* mausoleum. He then began planning his return to Rome. There, despite being the last man standing in the most recent contest of late Republican warlords, he remained highly unpopular with the *optimates* who criticized his reticence to incorporate Egypt as a new Roman province, and the length of time he was staying there.

First though he had two more matters to deal with in the east. In the first instance he travelled to Judea where he thanked the Jewish allies who had supported him during the Alexandrian War. Then he received word that the new Bosporan king, Pharnaces II son of Mithridates, had used the distraction of the Alexandrian War to invade Anatolia. Caesar knew the last thing the Romans wanted was another Mithridatic War and rushed north where he crushed the Pontic forces. In his own words to the Senate after his victory, he came, saw and conquered (*veni, vidi, vici*).

It was now well into 47 BC and Caesar was at last free to turn his full attention to Rome. He arrived back in Italy in September, leaving three veteran legions to protect Cleopatra and bringing back Arsinoe with him as a prisoner. He also gave Cyprus back to Egypt, which made him even more unpopular with the *optimates*. He was now dictator again, having already been appointed twice in his absence, and now appointed Mark Antony as his official deputy who received the title of Master of Horse. The latter had returned to Italy soon after Pharsalus and had been the effective ruler in Rome on Caesar's behalf since 47 BC. He lacked Caesar's leadership skills however and was soon facing rebellious Caesarian legionaries awaiting their discharge after the civil war, and rioting in Rome by disgruntled *optimates*.

Rome and Africa

Caesar's arrival in the Republican capital at the beginning of October was well-timed and the dictator soon restored order in Rome, though the mutinous soldiers were a different matter. They were still demanding their release from service so Caesar set out to address them directly. Here he listened to their grievances and then, calling them citizens rather than comrades as he had so many times before, dismissed them out of hand, promising they would receive their promised rewards in good time. This shocked them and most begged to be returned to service which Caesar, with mock reluctance, agreed to.

He now moved against the last bastion of Pompeian supporters, led by Cato, who had fled to the province of Africa. As usual he moved quickly, ordering the six legions and 2,000 allied cavalrymen of his army to take only the most essential baggage. They set sail from Sicily on the 25th of December. The fleet became scattered on the journey and when he landed near the enemy-held port of Hadrumentum south of Carthage he only had 3,500 legionaries and 150 cavalry with him. He demanded the town surrender but when ignored moved on, keen to seek out a meeting engagement to bring this new phase of civil war to a rapid end.

First he seized the ports of Ruspina and Little Leptis to allow the rest of his army to arrive. Within days he had three whole legions ready for operations and marched them inland to gather supplies. While out foraging this column was ambushed by the Pompeian commander Labienus with a force of local light troops, including the famous Numidian skirmishing cavalry. Soon Caesar was surrounded and further Pompeian troops arrived under Marcus Petreius, Gnaeus Calpurnius Psio, Quintus Caecilius Metellus Scipio and the Numidian king Juba I. Eventually Caesar was able to extricate his force but only after suffering heavy casualties. He knew he was lucky not to have been annihilated, and returned to Ruspina to begin training new recruits to replace those fallen in battle. He was still outnumbered by the *optimates* however and chose to remain in place until further reinforcements arrived in the form of his veteran *legios* XIII *Gemina* and XIV, 800 more allied cavalry and 1,000 skirmishing archers. The balance of power was further tipped towards parity when Juba had to return to Numidia to fend off a *populares-inspired* Mauretanian invasion.

Caesar now moved on to the offensive once more, advancing out of Ruspina on the 7th of November. However the Pompeian forces, now led solely by Scipio, declined battle. Caesar pressed on, now joined by two more legions including his elite *legio* X, and set up camp at Uzita. Again the Pompeians avoided battle so he pressed on southeast to Aggar. There he was joined by more reinforcements in February 46 BC and decided now was the time to force the enemy to battle. He knew he needed level ground with defended flanks to negate the *optimates* particular strength in cavalry. Scouting ahead he found that the nearby port city of Thapsus was an ideal location as it could only be approached by two isthmuses on either side of a very wide lagoon. His strategy was to advance on its Pompeian garrison along one isthmus and draw Scipio after him. To protect his rear he built a strong marching camp at the head of this strip as he passed, manning it with three cohorts. This would enable him to engage Scipio at the time of his choosing. He then invested Thapsus and waited for the *optimates* relief force to arrive.

Scipio promptly fell for the trap. Arriving at the head of the isthmus he found it blocked by the marching camp and withdrew to the shores of the lake where he built his own camp. Caesar now had him trapped and pounced immediately. Scipio had no choice but to accept battle as his line of retreat was blocked by the lake. He formed his legionaries in front of the palisade of his camp, with elephants he'd been left by Juba on his wings. Caesar countered with his usual three lines, deploying his skirmishers and an extra fourth line of legionaries on the flanks to counter the elephants.

When the battle opened Caesar's archers immediately targeted the elephants who panicked and started to trample their own men. Meanwhile a separate elephant charge into Caesar's center hit the veteran *legio* V *Alaudae* who fought so bravely that from that point their legionary symbol was an elephant. Across the wider battlefield Caesar's better troops were soon triumphant, and the battle was quickly over. When the Pompeian legionaries tried to surrender many were cut down where they stood, the army losing over 10,000 men to Caesar's alleged 50. Thapsus fell soon after and the Pompeian cause in Africa was lost. Pompey's two sons Gnaeus Pompeius and Sextus Pompeius fled to Spain where opposition to Caesar was again emerging. However Cato, Scipio and Juba took their own lives. Caesar then annexed Numidia and returned to Rome, victorious once more.

Triumph and Spain

Caesar arrived back in July 46 BC to huge acclamation, being awarded no less than four triumphs in one go for his exploits in Gaul, Egypt, Asia, and over Juba in Africa (the leading role of the Pompeians in the last campaign was glossed over). The celebrations were enormous in scale and lasted from the 21st of September through to the 2nd of October. During them various parades took place in which his famous captives, including Arsinoe, Juba's infant son and the once mighty Vercingetorix, were forced to participate. The latter was brutally strangled to death at the end of the Gallic parade in the traditional Roman way, though Arsinoe and the baby were spared during their parades. Caesar's celebrations made him even more wildly popular with the popular classes in Rome, the only jarring note being shock on the part of some at the sheer scale of bloodshed during the gladiator contests. A particular complaint was that he continued to carry out his daily work as dictator while watching the shows.

In late 46 BC Caesar's popularity was seriously put to the test when Cleopatra and her co-regent Ptolemy XIV visited Rome. She had already given birth to their son in June 47 BC, who she named Ptolemy XV Caesarion and announced as her heir. The visit was treated as royal in every sense. Scandalously she was even installed in Caesar's fine new home on the Janiculum Hill, this despite the fact that Caesar was still married to Calpurnia, and welcomed as a 'friend and ally of the Roman people'. Cleopatra was soon widely acknowledged as his mistress. In Caesar's villa she hosted a number of symposia for the great and the good of Rome.

He raised more eyebrows by next building a temple to his 'ancestor' Venus Genetrix to celebrate his victory over Pompey. This included a statue of Alexander the Great's horse Bucephalus outside, a clear statement of ambition on Caesar's part. However it was what he installed inside that proved even more controversial, namely a statue of Cleopatra in the form of Isis, immediately next to the statue of Venus. This was very un-Roman, troubling even his most ardent *populares* supporters. He also began placing statues of himself across Rome, one of them specifically linking himself to Alexander.

Caesar started a **building programme in Rome**, favouring a Graeco-Egyptian style. This included a new grand temple in the forum. It was also now that he created the new Julian calendar in his role as Pontifex Maximus, almost certainly with the help of Cleopatra's astronomers. With its 365 days and leap years, it was to remain the standard calendar in the western world until superseded by the Gregorian Calendar in 1582. After his death the Senate voted that the month of his birth should be named after him, today's July.

Next Caesar started appointing a large number of new Senators given the legislative body had been severely depleted by the civil wars. From this point onwards it would have a big *populares* majority among a membership of over 900. He then had a piece of legislation passed which time limited a proconsul's period in office to ensure a provincial governor didn't have time to create a powerbase with which to oppose him in future. He also gave himself the title of Prefect of the Morals, allowing him to wield censorial powers which meant that no magistrate could challenge him in court on matters relating to public morality and the public finances. Coins were also struck in his name and with his likeness, and he was given the power to speak first in the Senate. He also rewarded the supporters he'd been unable to elevate to the Senate by increasing the number of magistrates. Finally in this burst of administrative reform, he set in train the reorganisation of the whole of the territory of the Republic and its provinces into the single integrated unit that would eventually emerge in the reign of Augustus as the Roman Empire.

With matters well in hand in Rome, in late November 46 BC Caesar moved to address the final Pompeian bastion in Spain. There two legions in Hispania Ulterior had declared for Gnaeus Pompeius and Sextus Pompeius earlier in the year and driven out Caesar's proconsul. The brothers then arrived there with the remains of the *optimates* army from Africa, along with the *legate* Labienus who had caused Caesar so much trouble at the beginning of the war in Africa. They raised one more legion from the African troops and locals and now set about securing the province, with Caesar's generals Quintus Fabius Maximus and Quintus Pedius looking on and refusing to risk battle.

Caesar decided to intervene in person, knowing that if he dealt with Pompey's sons the *optimates* cause should be lost for good. Taking two veteran legions with him, X *Equestris* and V *Alaudae*, together with the less experienced III *Gallica* and VI *Ferrata*, he marched 2,400 km in less than a month, arriving in the campaigning theatre in late December.

Caesar was able to stop any further *optimates* expansion in the province, but the Pompeius brothers and Labienus avoided a meeting engagement, just as Scipio had in Africa. However, after a number of skirmishers their legionaries started to desert and they realised they had to engage now or all was lost. The ensuing engagement, the battle of Munda, was Caesar's last and one of his most hard fought. Here he fielded eight legions, with four more from Spain joining the four that had travelled with him, together with 8,000 allied cavalry. The Republicans fielded 13 legions, though a number had suffered badly from desertion, along with 6,000 horse and 6,000 light foot. In the coming battle many of the Pompeians would fight with desperation, knowing that having already gone over to Caesar's side earlier in the civil wars and then re-joined the *optimates,* they could expect no mercy.

After a failed attempt to lure the Republicans into a trap Caesar ordered his troops into a general attack with the watchword Venus. Both armies fought toe-to-toe for eight hours, with all the commanders joining in the fighting. Caesar based himself on his right flank where he joined *legio* X again. Eventually this began to push back the Pompeian legion opposite, causing Gnaeus Pompeius to withdraw a legion from his own right flank to bolster his left. The weakened right flank was now exploited by Caesar's allied cavalry there, commanded by King Bogud of Mauritania, who wheeled round its furthest extremity and charged the Pompeian camp to the rear of their battle line. Labienus now ordered his own cavalry to the rear to counter Bogud's men, but the Pompeian legionaries – already heavily engaged and falling back on their left – thought Labienus was retreating and gradually broke, then fled in disorder. As usual Caesar pursued vigorously. A few of the Pompeians were able to make the safety of Munda, though not many. An estimated 30,000 were left dead on the battlefield, with all 13 of their legionary standards being captured. Caesar claimed that he lost only 1,000 men. Labienus fell himself, being granted a burial by Caesar, though the Pompeius brothers escaped. Gnaeus was later captured in a small engagement at the town of Lauro and executed, while Sextus survived, much later causing a rebellion in Sicily. There he was finally defeated by Marcus Agrippa and executed by Mark Antony in Asia in 35 BC. Back in Spain, after the battle Caesar left Maximus to invest Munda and moved to restore the wider province, dealing severely with any surviving *optimates*.

Caesar then returned to Rome again, where he was the victor once more. However, now for the first time he seriously overplayed his hand, with Plutarch (*Lives*, Caesar, 56) saying:

> ...the triumph he celebrated...displeased the Romans more than any other. For he had not defeated foreign generals or barbarian kings, but had destroyed the sons and family of one of the greatest men of Rome, who had met with misfortune, and it was not proper for him to lead a procession of celebration of the calamities of his country, rejoicing in things for which no other defence could be made to Gods or men than that they had been done out of necessity.

Caesar carried on with his pro-*populares* reforms regardless. However, he continued to take steps to ensure he remained in power as long as he wanted to, and on his own terms. He had already stepped down as the sole consul in October 45 BC to prepare for the Spanish campaign, making sure two supporters would be elected to replace him for the remainder of the year. Though in theory this restored the joint-consulship as the primary political executive in the Republic, he remained dictator. In effect, the consuls and Senate could therefore only act on his say so. Then in February 44 BC he was appointed dictator for life, which made him an absolute monarch in all but name. He then passed a law allowing him to appoint all magistrates in 43 BC, and consuls and tribunes in 42 BC. This was draconian indeed, though the context was to secure his political 'rear' for his next foreign campaign. Never one to rest on his considerable laurels, this was to be an invasion of the mighty Parthian empire in the east, the nemesis of his one-time triumvir colleague Crassus. For this Caesar planned to take an enormous force of 16 legions and 10,000 allied cavalry.

For many in Rome, despite the excesses of his triumphs and favouring of Cleopatra, Caesar's time as dictator was a prosperous one. Unlike the civil strife that marred the era of Marius and Sulla, most of the civil war campaigning in Caesar's time was abroad in Macedonia, Greece, Africa and Spain. There is also no doubt that the Roman popular classes loved a winner, particularly one who so overtly championed the *populares* cause. However, Caesar's ascension to a position of absolute authority over the political classes in Rome was jarring to many of the capital's leading senators and equestrians. This was particularly the case with regard to the *optimates*, most of whose leaders had already perished or were in exile. Caesar's recent Pompeian triumph only exacerbated the issue. The Roman nobility was very proud of their forebears having thrown off the fetters of the monarchy of Tarquin the Proud in 509 BC. Many felt it was time to do so again.

Assassination

Plotting to assassinate Caesar began while he was away in Spain. His subsequent triumph, and being made dictator for life, then acted as the twin catalysts that finally drove his enemies, and even some former supporters, to act. The conspiracy featured more than 60 senators and was led by Gaius Cassius Longinus (best known to posterity as Cassius), Decimus Junius Brutus Albinus and Marcus Junius Brutus (best known as Brutus). The group styled themselves Liberators and aimed to restore normal consular-led senatorial governance to the Republic. After considering a number of plans of action, they decided to kill Caesar in the Senate itself where they could hide daggers under their heavy togas.

Opportunity soon presented itself. On the Ides of March (15th of March) 44 BC the dictator was set to preside over a session of the Senate. At the time this was being held in the Curia of

The Senate curia in the forum, Rome. Caesar was actually assassinated in the Curia of Pompey within the larger Theatre of Pompey, as the actual Senate building was being renovated at the time.

Pompey within the larger Theatre of Pompey, given Caesar was having a new Senate House built to replace the previous Curia Hostilia which had burned down in 53 BC. Caesar is said to have been given a number of warnings about his impending demise, including by Calpurnia following a bad dream, his doctors who warned him of his ill health, and by religious sacrifices which had produced bad omens, including the famous omen immortalized by Shakespeare regarding the Ides of March. However, he chose to ignore them and set off as normal.

While Caesar was travelling Mark Antony tried to intercept him, having heard in the night that an attack on Caesar was being planned. However the plotters had planned for this and when he arrived at the steps of Pompey's Theatre one of the Liberators, either Brutus Albinus or Caesar's former *legate* Gaius Trebonius, detained him long enough for the deed to be carried out.

Plutarch (*Lives*, Caesar, 60) says that when Caesar entered the Senate chamber the members rose out of respect for him. Then, as he sat, some of the conspirators fanned out behind his chair, while others approached to support the supposed petition of their fellow plotter Tillius Cimber to allow his exiled brother to be recalled to Rome. He rebuffed them, suspecting nothing, but then Cimber pulled Caesar's toga down by the neck. This was the signal to strike, with Publius Servilius Casca Longus, the Tribune of the People, stabbing him in the neck first. This was a non-mortal blow and, after a shocked pause, the other conspirators joined in. He was allegedly stabbed 23 times and even though he tried to get away there was no escape, he eventually being blinded by his own blood. Even if he had managed to fight his way out it would have been to no avail according to Suetonius (*The Twelve Caesars*, Julius Caesar, 82) who says the surgeon Antistius in his autopsy declared the second wound, to his chest, was ultimately the fatal one. Caesar's last act was to pull his toga over his head when he saw Brutus among the assassins, according to Plutarch (*Lives*, Caesar, 66).

Immediately after the murder Brutus moved forward to say something, but his fellow conspirators panicked and fled. When some of them arrived in the forum they proclaimed Rome to be free of a tyrannical monarch once more. They were met with a shocked silence by the crowd and knew immediately how badly they had judged the popular mood. Meanwhile, Mark Antony had fled the Theatre of Pompey as soon as he had heard the commotion inside. He stayed in hiding for a short while, before emerging to take centre stage in all that followed. Caesar's body was left where it fell for three hours until magistrates arrived to organise its removal. The Liberators may have thought their deed had saved the Republic. Instead, it initiated its demise.

CONCLUSION

As the reader will determine from the above biography of Caesar's life and times, his story is truly astonishing. It stands up against that of any of the other great figure of world history. Yet his legacy was even more important, both in the ancient world and subsequently. Both are considered here, before I finally make the case for why Caesar was Rome's greatest warlord.

Caesar's Contemporary Legacy

Caesar's funeral ceremony also sounded the death knell of the Republic. The Senate, seeking to encourage almost immediate reconciliation between the *optimates* and *populares*, voted that it should be public. The event duly took place on the 18th of March, with Mark Antony giving the eulogy from the *rostra* in the forum. There he reminded the huge crowd, which included thousands of Caesar's veterans, of the dictator's many achievements. He then read Caesar's will, which included the gift of a huge new garden complex along the Tiber for the citizens of Rome, and 75 *denarii* for each Roman citizen (Caesar also naming Octavian as his sole heir). Mark Anthony then showed off Caesar's bloody toga, before the body was finally lifted up by magistrates to be carried to a site next to the tomb of his daughter Julia on the Campus Martia where it was due to be cremated and interred. The crowd would have none of it however, having been whipped into a frenzy by Mark Antony. They seized the body and cremated it there and then on a pyre built in front of the *rostra*. Veterans and citizens alike threw their precious goods into the huge blaze as a sign of their grief, with the flames quickly spinning out of control. In short order many of the buildings in the forum were badly damaged.

Violence now erupted against the *optimates*, with the huge funeral crowd turning into a rampaging mob that attacked the houses of Cassius, Brutus and others. In the frenzy Caesar's loyal supporter Helvius Cinna was killed by rioters who mistook him for the plotter Cornelius Cinna. It took days for order to be restored in the capital, by which time Caesar's legacy as the leading man of Rome murdered by bitter *optimates* was firmly established. On the site of his cremation the Temple of Caesar was later erected on the eastern side of the main square of the forum, featuring a life-size wax statue of the dictator. He was also later deified in 42 BC as the Divine Julius, this setting a pattern for the Emperors of the Roman Empire. His immediate legacy however was the new civil war that broke out almost immediately after his death.

The first act here was the flight of the leading *optimates*, including Cassius and Brutus, to Greece to avoid the anger of the Roman mob. The *populares* had already dealt with key plot leader Decimus Junius Brutus Albinus who initially fled north to Cisalpine Gaul where he survived a number of attempts to defeat him, only to be executed by a Gallic chief loyal to Caesar when he tried to reach Greece. There Cassius and Brutus were raising an enormous army which Mark Antony in Italy countered by gathering an equally large force using the immense wealth Caesar's own war chest. He legitimised his actions by saying he was acting in the name of Caesar. Then, on the 27th of November 43 BC the *lex Titia* law was passed which established the Second Triumvirate of Mark Antony, Octavian and Caesar's loyal commander Lepidus. This ensured the continued rule of the *populares*, with their first action being to reinstate the policy of proscription last used under Sulla. Soon those *optimates* still in Rome were being rounded up and executed. Their estates and wealth were then confiscated to fund the raising of even more new *populares* legions. Eventually the triumvirate took the war to the *optimates* in Greece where Cassius and Brutus were heavily defeated at the battle of Philippi by Mark Antony and Octavian in October 42 BC. Both Cassius and Brutus committed suicide in the aftermath.

However, as with the First Triumvirate, the second was not to last. In the mid 30s BC Octavian accused Lepidus of trying to usurp power, stripping him of all titles and exiling him after most of his troops defected to Octavian. Meanwhile Mark Antony campaigned in the east, where he suffered a big defeat in an invasion of Parthia after over extending his lines of supply. He now increasingly came under the influence of Cleopatra in Egypt with whom he formed an alliance. He still styled himself triumvir even after the time period agreed in the *lex Titia* expired in 33 BC. A new and final civil war soon broke out between himself with Cleopatra against Octavian. The latter was the ultimate victor at the climactic battle of Actium in 31 BC, his fleet under Marcus Agrippa destroying that of Mark Antony and Cleopatra who fled to Egypt and later famously committed suicide in 30 BC. This left Octavian as the last man standing after the turbulent civil wars that had plagued Rome throughout the 1st century BC. He was already able to call himself *Divi Filius* (son of a god) given Caesar's deification, and by 27 BC the Senate was calling him Caesar Augustus. The Republic was no more, and the Roman Empire now came into being.

Caesar's Legacy Today

For the Romans the greatest Imperial figure was Augustus, the first Emperor. His enormous success set the standard by which all future Emperor's measured themselves. This also set a standard when, later in the Empire, the concept of senior and junior

Emperors was introduced. The former were called Augustus and the latter Caesar.

In the post-Roman world however this was reversed, with Caesar and his epic story being that by which rulers measured themselves. This was particularly the case from the time of the later Middle Ages and Renaissance, perhaps peaking with William Shakespeare's contemporary blockbuster *Julius Caesar*.

It was Caesar who gave his name to the rulers of the Russian and Slavic world with their Tsars, and to the Germanic Kaiser. And it was Caesar on whom future would-be conquerors styled themselves, for example the Ottoman Sultan Mehmed II who was the ultimate nemesis of the Roman Empire when he finally captured the Byzantine capital of Constantinople in 1453, Charles VIII of France who ordered a translation of *The Conquest of Gaul*, and the Holy Roman Emperor Charles V who ordered a map to be made of France to better understand Caesar's Gallic wars. Meanwhile, the contemporary Ottoman Sultan Suleiman the Magnificent translated Caesar's commentaries into Turkish and catalogued the surviving editions. Later, the French kings Henry IV, Louis XIII and Louis XIV all had Caesar's commentaries translated into French.

Into the 19th century Napoleon Bonaparte studied not only Caesar's military prowess but also his skill as a strategic communicator, while later in the century his style of leadership inspired a political ideology called Caesarism based on unrestricted rule by a charismatic strongman. One adherent, unsurprisingly, was Benito Mussolini.

More broadly in terms of Caesar's legacy, there was the Julian calendar used throughout the western world until the advent of the Gregorian calendar in 1582. Additionally, as detailed in the Introduction, his campaigning in Spain and conquests in Gaul facilitated the spread of the Latin language and Roman law which still influence linguistics and legal systems there to this day. For all of the reason set out above we thus still live in the shadow of this great figure of the ancient world.

Rome's Greatest Warlord?

As set out in the Introduction, the military reforms of Marius in 107 BC in the context of the Cimbrian War created a new style of ubiquitous legion. Each included all of the specialists in its ranks needed to campaign in enemy territory, meaning they could operate independent of long lines of supply. This was specifically seen with Caesar's invasion of Macedonia and Greece when bringing Pompey to battle, and later in the Alexandrian War and in North Africa. These formations were very mobile and allowed the various military leaders to build private armies of multiple legions. Marius also removed the property requirement to serve as a legionary, allowing the lower end of Roman society to sign up for front line service for the first time. These troops then proved very loyal to their leaders given they were totally reliant on them for their pay, and when on campaign the opportunity for plunder, especially in the east. This combination of new, easily combined legions who were very loyal to their army leaders thus allowed the evolution of the Roman military commander of the late Republic into a new style of warlord, often operating independently of the Republican state.

Of these the candidates to be the greatest are easy to list. Think of Marius himself, Sulla, Cinna, Crassus, Pompey, Caesar, Mark Antony, the Liberators, Lepidus, and finally Octavian and his general Marcus Agrippa. All were successful to a greater or lesser extent. All made their mark on the late Republic. All are significant figures in wider world history. However, Caesar also had one further factor in his favour. This was through his creation of so many new legions, more so than any of his opponents. The key factor here was his policy of promoting the centurions of his existing legions to be the new senior officers of those newly recruited, and the senior legionaries of the existing formations to be the centurions of the new. This made them even more loyal, often fanatically so.

All of the above listed late Republican warlords displayed a combination of leadership traits. These included personal

Julius Caesar: statesman, warlord and dictator.

bravery, the ability to be brutal when necessary, strategic and tactical prowess, the ability to communicate with audiences high and low and great and small, that most Roman of traits grit which meant they kept coming back, the charisma to inspire on a large scale, and decisiveness. Caesar was the only one who had them all, and because of this he was the warlord who was the most constantly, and conspicuously, successful. That is why he should be considered Rome's greatest warlord.

ANCIENT SOURCES

Julius Caesar, *The Conquest of Gaul*. 1951. Handford, S.A., London: Penguin.

Plutarch, *Lives of the Noble Greeks and Romans*. 2013. Clough, A. H. Oxford: Benediction Classics.

Polyaenus, *Stratagems*. 2010. Shepherd, F. R. S. Michigan: Gale ECCO.

Suetonius, *The Twelve Caesars*, 1957. Graves, R. London: Penguin.

FURTHER READING

Bishop, M. C. (2017). *Gladiators: Fighting to the Death in Ancient Rome.* Casemate Publishers.

Cowan, R. (2003). *Roman Legionary 58 BC–AD 69.* Osprey Publishing.

Elliott, S. (2016). *Sea Eagles of Empire: The Classis Britannica and the Battles for Britain.* History Press.

Elliott, S. (2018). *Roman Legionaries: Soldiers of Empire.* Casemate Publishers.

Goldsworthy, A. (2006). *Caesar.* W&N.

Haywood, J. (2009). *The Historical Atlas of the Celtic World.* Thames & Hudson.

Holland, T. (2004). *Rubicon: The Triumph and Tragedy of the Roman Republic.* Abacus.

Moorhead S. and Stuttard, D. (2012). *The Romans Who Shaped Britain.* Thames & Hudson.

Spawforth, T. (2018). *The Story of Greece and Rome.* Yale University Press.

ACKNOWLEDGEMENTS

I would like to thank the many people who have helped make *Julius Caesar: Rome's Greatest Warlord* possible. Specifically, as always Professor Andrew Lambert of the War Studies Department at KCL, Dr Andrew Gardner at UCL's Institute of Archaeology and Dr Steve Willis at the University of Kent. All continue to give much appreciated encouragement and guidance with regard to my writing projects. Next, my publisher Casemate Publishers, and specifically Ruth Sheppard and Isobel Nettleton there. Also Professor Sir Barry Cunliffe of the School of Archaeology at Oxford University, and Professor Martin Millett at the Faculty of Classics, Cambridge University. Next, my patient proof reader and lovely wife Sara, and my dad John Elliott for being my partner in crime in various escapades researching this book. As with all of my literary work, all have contributed greatly and freely, enabling this work to reach fruition. Finally of course I would like to thank my family, especially my tolerant wife Sara once again and children Alex and Lizzie.

INDEX